D1561561

PROMETHEUS

Archetypal Image of Human Existence

BOLLINGEN SERIES LXV · I

Carl Kerényi

PROMETHEUS

Archetypal Image of Human Existence

TRANSLATED FROM THE GERMAN BY
Ralph Manheim

BOLLINGEN SERIES LXV · I

PRINCETON UNIVERSITY PRESS
PRINCETON, NEW JERSEY

Published by Princeton University Press, 41 William Street, Princeton,
New Jersey 08540
In the United Kingdom: Princeton University Press, Chichester, West Sussex

THIS IS VOLUME ONE IN A GROUP OF STUDIES OF *Archetypal Images of Greek
Religion* WHICH CONSTITUTE THE SIXTY-FIFTH PUBLICATION IN A SERIES
SPONSORED AND PUBLISHED BY BOLLINGEN FOUNDATION

Translated from *Prometheus: Die menschliche Existenz in griechischer Deutung,*
published by Rowohlt Verlag, Hamburg, copyright © 1959 Rhein-Verlag AG, Zurich.
Earlier version: *Prometheus: Das griechische Mythologem von der menschlichen
Existenz,* copyright © 1946 Rhein-Verlag AG, Zurich

Library of Congress Catalogue Card Number: 59-13516
ISBN 0-691-01907-X (pbk.)

Princeton University Press books are printed on acid-free paper and meet the
guidelines for permanence and durability of the Committee on Production Guidelines
for Book Longevity of the Council on Library Resources

First Princeton Paperback printing, in the Mythos series, 1997

http://pup.princeton.edu

Printed in the United States of America

1 3 5 7 9 10 8 6 4 2

CONTENTS

LIST OF PLATES

[I

THE PRESENT essay, like others of my books, particularly those devoted to the retelling of Greek mythology, *The Gods of the Greeks* and *The Heroes of the Greeks*, emphasizes the mythological aspect of Greek religion. But Archetypal Images in Greek Religion, the series of monographs of which this essay is the first, puts greater emphasis on a dimension that was treated only implicitly in the above-mentioned works. These were "an experimental attempt to translate the mythology of the Greeks back, to some extent at least, into its original medium, into mythological storytelling."[1] Storytelling moves in the dimension of language, of the "word," as the Greek tongue stresses by terming this particular kind of narrative, dealing largely with the gods and heroes, *mythos*, "word," and *mythología*, "storytelling."

But "word" and "storytelling," myth and mythology, have their full meaning only in the broader dimension of existence as a whole, of Greek existence in the case of Greek mythology. Moreover, thanks to their form as stories, the myths—whether committed to writing or not—were a part of Greek literature. As works of literature, they were studied chiefly by classical scholars and, as rendered in works of art, by classical archaeologists. The aim I have in mind[2] is a classical scholarship which through research comes closer to a science of Greek and Roman existence than has formerly been the case. The meaning of the myths, wherever they occur in a living state and not merely as works of literature, has to do with existence. The contention that this

1. *The Gods of the Greeks*, p. 4.
2. Cf. *Apollon; Niobe; Griechische Miniaturen.*

xi

was so among the Greeks is no gratuitous hypothesis: the important role of mythology, the continuous retelling of the myths in Greek literature and art, cannot be explained by mere "love of storytelling." If this had been the case, Greek literature would be far richer in purely human themes than we know it to be.

To meet our aim, it will be necessary to increase our knowledge of the correspondences between Greek mythology and Greek existence and of course between Greek mythology, which of all the mythologies in the world is closest to us, and all existence. It requires no great interpretive skill to find such images of existence in Greek mythology. In the great literatures of the West the poets who invoked the figures of Greek mythology could always count on a certain degree of transparency in these figures. And this transparency is by no means limited to the persons of mythology and their stories, but—if they really correspond to existence—extends to existence itself, or at least to Greek existence, which is in a way related to our existence since it is built upon the same foundations.

Up until now insufficient attention has been paid to the correspondence between mythology and existence in the world of the Greeks on which our world, that of Western civilization, is based. This may be explained by the fragmentary form in which Greek mythology has come down to us: almost always the myths, as they reach us, are severed from their bond with the living religion, the cult, and life itself, and show a predominantly literary and artistic character. The significance that mythology can have within existence as a whole has been brought out by observers—not necessarily ethnologists—who have somewhere encountered it in a living state. The classic example is that of Sir George Grey, who was sent to New Zealand in 1845 by the British government, and who shortly thereafter became Governor

General. In 1855 he published his *Polynesian Mythology and Ancient Traditional History of the New Zealand Race, as furnished by Their Priests and Chiefs.* I have quoted from his preface in the introduction to *The Gods of the Greeks.* Here I must do so once again. His report runs:

"When I arrived . . . , I found Her Majesty's native subjects engaged in hostilities with the Queen's troops, against whom they had up to that time contended with considerable success; so much discontent also prevailed generally amongst the native population, that where disturbances had not yet taken place, there was too much reason to apprehend they would soon break out, as they shortly afterwards did, in several parts of the Islands.

"I soon perceived that I could neither successfully govern, nor hope to conciliate, a numerous and turbulent people, with whose language, manners, customs, religion, and modes of thought I was quite unacquainted. In order to redress their grievances, and apply remedies, which would neither wound their feelings, nor militate against their prejudices, it was necessary that I should be able thoroughly to understand their complaints; and to win their confidence and regard, it was also requisite that I should be able at all times, and in all places, patiently to listen to the tales of their wrongs or sufferings, and, even if I could not assist them, to give them a kind reply, couched in such terms as should leave no doubt on their minds that I clearly understood and felt for them, and was really well disposed towards them. . . .

"These reasons, and others of equal force, made me feel it to be my duty to make myself acquainted, with the least possible delay, with the language of the New Zealanders, as also with their manners, customs, and prejudices. But I soon found that this was a far more difficult matter than I had first supposed. The language of the New

Zealanders is a very difficult one to understand thoroughly: there was then no dictionary of it published (unless a vocabulary can be so called); there were no books published in the language, which would enable me to study its construction; it varied altogether in form from any of the ancient or modern languages which I knew; and my thoughts and time were so occupied with the cares of the government of a country then pressed upon by many difficulties, and with a formidable rebellion raging in it, that I could find but very few hours to devote to the acquisition of an unwritten and difficult language. I, however, did my best, and cheerfully devoted all my spare moments to a task, the accomplishment of which was necessary to enable me to perform properly every duty to my country and to the people I was appointed to govern.

"Soon, however, a new and quite unexpected difficulty presented itself. On the side of the rebel party were engaged, either openly or covertly, some of the oldest, least civilised, and most influential chiefs in the Islands. With them I had either personally, or by written communications, to discuss questions which involved peace or war, and on which the whole future of the Islands and of the native race depended, so that it was in the highest degree essential that I should fully and entirely comprehend their thoughts and intentions, and that they should not in any way misunderstand the nature of the engagements into which I entered with them.

"To my surprise, however, I found that these chiefs, either in their speeches to me, or in their letters, frequently quoted, in explanation of their views and intentions, fragments of ancient poems or proverbs, or made allusions which rested on an ancient system of mythology; and although it was clear that the most important parts of their communications were embodied in these figurative forms, the interpreters were quite at fault, they could then rarely (if ever) translate the poems or explain the allusions, and there was no publication in existence which threw any light upon these subjects, or which gave the meaning of the great mass of the words which the natives upon such occasions made use of; so that I was compelled to content myself with a short general statement of what some other native believed that the writer of the letter intended to convey as his meaning by the fragment of the poem he had quoted, or by the allusions he had made. I should add, that even the great majority of the young Christian natives were quite as much at fault on these subjects as were the European interpreters.

"Clearly, however, I could not, as Governor of the country, permit so close a veil to remain drawn between myself and the aged and influential chiefs, whom it was my duty to attach to British interests and to the British race, whose regard and confidence, as also that of their tribes, it was my desire to secure, and with whom it was necessary that I should hold the most unrestricted intercourse. Only one thing could, under such circumstances, be done, and that was to acquaint myself with the ancient language of the country, to collect its traditional poems and legends, to induce their priests to impart to me their mythology, and to study their proverbs. For more than eight years I devoted a great part of my available time to these pursuits. Indeed I worked at this duty in my spare moments in every part of the country I traversed, and during my many voyages from portion to portion of the Islands. I was also always accompanied by natives, and still at every possible interval pursued my inquiries into these subjects . . ." (pp. iii–viii).

[2

THERE is a certain similarity between the role of mythology among the Maoris of New Zealand and among the Greeks, even if we consider only its literary significance. Those of us who have gone through humanistic studies recall having had the same experience as the British Governor General; in order to understand the ancient Greeks, we had to learn not only their language but their mythology as well. In his lecture on "Freud and the Future" Thomas Mann aptly characterized life in the days when mythology was still alive as a "quotation-like life." "Ancient life and its consciousness of itself," he wrote, "were different from ours, less exclusive, less sharply delimited. It was, one might say, open toward the past, taking up many past things which it repeated in the present so that they were 'there again.' The Spanish philosopher Ortega y Gasset has expressed this by saying that the ancient, before doing anything, took a step backward like the bullfighter poising himself for the death stroke. In the past, says Ortega, he sought a model into which he slipped as into a diving bell before flinging himself, at once protected and distorted, into the problems of the present." ³ A life of this sort is perfectly imaginable; ancient history contains stereotyped cases of it, and we can disclose it with certainty as the preliminary stage and premise of a literature and art full of mythological "quotations." It is only because classical scholarship from the very start derived its orientation from literature that this so obvious insight has not been generally accepted.

But if we wish to show this significance of Greek myths by con-

3. Thomas Mann, *Freud und die Zukunft,* p. 33. (Cf. Ortega y Gasset, *The Revolt of the Masses,* p. 173.)

crete examples and to restore their existential dimension and thereby their transparency toward human existence, we cannot content ourselves with a general knowledge, however self-evident. We must make use of the observations of the ethnologists to define the nature of the correspondence between myth and existence clearly and precisely, and then cite sure examples of it from Greek mythology. The approach may be based on the researches among the Cora Indians of K. T. Preuss, who summarized his findings in a study of the religious content of the myths,[4] in so far as the findings applied to a correspondence between myths and ritual. In defining this correspondence as it relates to "existence," to the life of man, indeed to all life in the world of men, he did not limit himself to the rites, but spoke of the "present conditions and constantly recurrent phenomena," which were certified "by a unique event in the primordial era." Still more precise and meticulous is the formulation of Bronislaw Malinowski in his little book *Myth in Primitive Psychology,* in which he records his observations in the Trobriand Islands, north of New Guinea. I have quoted him in the foreword to the volume on the science of mythology (p. 7), written in collaboration with C. G. Jung, but here I must do so at greater length:

"Myth as it exists in a savage community, that is, in its living primitive form, is not merely a story told but a reality lived. It is not of the nature of fiction, such as we read today in a novel, but it is a living reality, believed to have once happened in primeval times, and continuing ever since to influence the world and human destinies. This myth is to the savage what, to a fully believing Christian, is the Biblical story of Creation, of the Fall, of the Redemption by Christ's sacrifice on the Cross. As our sacred story lives in our ritual, in our

4. K. T. Preuss, *Der religiöse Gehalt der Mythen.*

morality, as it governs our faith and controls our conduct, even so does his myth for the savage . . ." (p. 21).

"I maintain that there exists a special class of stories, regarded as sacred, embodied in ritual, morals, and social organization, and which form an integral and active part in primitive culture. These stories live not by idle interest, not as fictitious or even as true narratives; but are to the natives a statement of a primeval, greater, and more relevant reality, by which the present life, fates, and activities of mankind are determined, the knowledge of which supplies man with the motive for ritual and moral actions, as well as with indications as to how to perform them" (p. 39).

For a correspondence such as this between "a primeval, greater, and more relevant reality" and "the present life, fates, and activities of mankind," between "myth" and "existence," the language of the English Platonists possessed a terminology which has also been taken up in part by a trend in modern psychology: *archetypal* for the original and timeless, *ectypal* for what corresponds to it in our temporal world. According to the *Century Dictionary*,[5] the *ectypal world* is "the phenomenal world, the world of sense, as distinguished from the archetypal . . . world." C. G. Jung's choice of the word *"Archetyp"* in his psychological theory had its background in our Western culture and its humanistic tradition.[6] In my own choice of the term "archetypal" Jung's psychological explanation of the phenomenon was not the only factor. Of course, by using the term, I establish a connection between my investigations and modern psychology. But I should like to remind the reader that in my essay on the "Divine Child," written before my meeting with C. G. Jung, I managed quite well without the term

---

5. Vol. II (1900). The definition was called to my attention by R. F. C. Hull.
6. Kerényi, *Umgang mit Göttlichem*, p. 52.

"archetypal." My actual title was "The Primordial Child in Primordial Times." This was still rather long; "archetypal" is a good deal shorter. Even so, I should not have used the word here if it had been employed *only* in psychology. Fortunately—and to me this was the decisive factor—the term "archetypal" had already been used in the languages of the Western nations to designate a phenomenon with which any empirical investigation of mythology has to deal. A historical foundation for the parallel observed by ethnologists between the world of the gods and the "ectypal world" is provided by the Greek tradition. The attributes and actions of certain of the Greek gods are reflected in clearly definable realms of existence—or conversely the latter are reflected in the divine figures and the images and imagery of mythology.

Thus I speak of "archetypal images" not on the basis of any explanatory theory but *phenomenologically*, describing mythology and tracing it back to its foundation in Greek existence. But here I should like to make it very clear that I do not take the word "existence" from existentialist philosophy [7]—that I do not use it in a strictly "existentialist" sense—but, like "archetypal," from the *language*, which I believe is common to all of us in Western civilization. My work is not "existentialist" any more than my *Gods of the Greeks* and *Heroes of the Greeks* are "Jungian mythology." My research is limited by no psychological theory, nor, for that matter, is it one-sidedly influenced by the ideas on ancient religion of Sir James Frazer and most classical scholars. I have set forth my interpretation of the religion of the Greeks and Romans in a special work, published in 1940, a reworked English version [8] of which appeared in 1962.

7. See the Preface to my *Griechische Miniaturen*, pp. 5 f.
8. Kerényi, *The Religion of the Greeks and Romans*.

[3

T H E strict correspondence between myth and existence and, what amounts to the same thing, the archetypal character and existential significance of mythology were not deduced by the ethnologists from Greek reality as it has come down to us in the tradition. Though it is highly probable and almost self-evident that this relationship must have been the same among the Greeks as among the peoples in whom it has been possible to observe mythology in a living state, we shall regard it for the present as no more than a working hypothesis. A cogent example has not yet been named. But such an example exists. For what the ethnologist observes concerning the role of mythology among the inhabitants of the Trobriand Islands fits in exactly with the mythologem of the sacrifice of Prometheus, the primordial sacrifice of the Greeks. Malinowski had examined all the types of narratives prevailing among the natives, including those that only correspond to our "fairy tales," historical accounts, or legends. According to him the mark of the sacred tales or myths, for which the natives also have a special name, is precisely the parallel between "archetypal" and "ectypal."

And just this is the case with the example I have mentioned. For the Greeks the story of this sacrifice as told by Hesiod [9] was the statement of a great primordial reality which determined the subsequent existence and fate of mankind. Knowledge of this reality had provided the Greeks of the historical period with the theme—by then scarcely intelligible—of their most important sacrificial action and with the instructions for performing it. This example in itself makes it clear

9. Hesiod, *Theogony* 535–64.

that among the Greeks "mythology" started out with preliterary functions, formally identical with those it served in those other archaic
communities that Malinowski calls "savage" or "primitive." But in
connection with the strange story recorded by Hesiod, a fundamental
question arises: How could this wild, abstruse story of Prometheus
trying to deceive the gods with his sacrifice carry any force of convic-
tion for the Greeks?

In trying to answer this question we must consider the authority
carried by myths in societies (such as those observed by our ethnologists) where they were still alive. Though the relevance of myth
to the "ectypal world" is not always immediately discernible among
the Greeks, it is a characteristic fact that the poets were *especially*
attached to mythological subjects. It is true that ancient poets and
artists were generally more limited in their themes than those of a
later day. But this does not account for the still greater restrictions imposed on their treatment of mythological material. Restriction in the
treatment of mythological material was the earlier phenomenon, and
the poets and artists were very slow to free themselves from it. Regardless of whether this constraint was inward—springing from the poet's
own religious faith—or outward, imposed by the collectivity, in either
case it was rooted in the material itself. *For this was sacred material.*
And it was a *special function* to tell of the gods and heroes or portray
them. An unwritten law imposed restrictions. It is an anachronism to
suppose that the Greeks enjoyed complete poetic and artistic freedom
in respect to mythology.

Yet the Greeks as we know them were not so blindly devoted to a
faith as to carry a merely believed mythology about with them for
centuries unless it had some meaning for them. But the meaning was
not one that might readily have been formulated in other terms, as a

doctrine. Prometheus, founder of the sacrifice, was a cheat and a thief: these traits are at the bottom of all the stories that deal with him. The meaning of his strange sacrifice in which the gods were cheated out of the tasty morsels is simply this: that the sacrifice offered up by men is a sacrifice of foolhardy thieves, stealers of the divinity round about them—for the world of nature that surrounds them is divine—whose temerity brings immeasurable and unforeseen misfortune upon them. Is this conception merely primitive or might it not embody a wisdom concerning human existence that would be hard to express in other than mythological terms?

On the strength of his observations Malinowski denied both the symbolic and the etiological character of living mythology. "We can certainly discard all explanatory as well as all symbolic interpretations of these myths of origin," he writes. "The personages and beings which we find in them are what they appear to be on the surface, and not symbols of hidden realities. As to any explanatory [i.e., etiological] function of these myths, there is no problem which they cover, no curiosity which they satisfy, no theory which they contain" (p. 79).

Everything Malinowski says about the Melanesian myths of origin applies to the mythologem of the origin of the Greeks' main sacrifice and indeed to the whole Prometheus myth—except for the denial of its etiological character. For the story of the primordial sacrifice does seem to be etiological, that is, to indicate a cause: and it also satisfies a childlike curiosity. But to this end did it have to brand the principal sacrifice of the Greeks as a swindle? Here again Malinowski's contention is justified. But at least in the Greek myths there is something that goes beyond it, namely, the transparency that mythology takes on when considered in the light of the correspondence between "archetypal" and "ectypal," of the totality that *myth* and *existence* formed for the

Greeks. This is what we shall attempt to do for the Prometheus myth in the present volume.

[4

W E usually come to mythology through the poets, and the best approach to it is through the poets who are closest to us. By their treatment of the material they are able to communicate to us not only the content of the myths but also the *experience* of mythology. For it is not only the natural sciences that stand in need of experience (in Greek, *empeiria*); the sciences that deal with creations of the spirit must be grounded in a kind of experience which gives them, if not an *empeiria*, at least a *peira*—a "testing" and "sampling," a minimum of experience of the spiritual occupation they are concerned with.

Peira toi mathēsios archa, says the Greek poet Alkman: "To test for yourself is the beginning of learning." [10] It is the poets who best enable us to sample long-dead mythologems. The Greek word *mythologēma* comes from *mythologein,* the verb meaning to engage in the activity of mythology—Greek *mythología*—an activity which, particularly in certain early periods of human history, can be compared to the other grave or playful activities of the mind. Apart from the content of the mythologems—in the present volume the mythologem of Prometheus—we shall be very much concerned with this activity of myth making. In this connection, of course, a good deal of importance will be attached to certain distinctive features of mythology which it does not necessarily share with poetry. One of these is that it is possible to consider mythology entirely from the standpoint of its substance. Then the mythologem becomes a movement, a development of a spe-

10. Fr. 67 in *Lyra graeca* (tr. Edmonds), I, 92–93.

cific content, and the best way in which we can deal with it is to follow the movement through the various traditions. This is something very different from merely recording the material that has come down to us and classifying it chronologically. Mythological lexicons and handbooks do just this; they excerpt the tradition and so reduce it to mere content. But originally the content was presented in poetic works. Our best guide will be the authors of such works.

Some of them entered into the living tradition. This is the case with the ancient poets. They were *mythológoi*. Narrators of myth, they remained within the framework of the mythologem, adhering to the broad outlines of earlier accounts. They repeated what they had heard and what was known to their hearers and readers. But by varying the theme, they set the mythologem in motion. Other poets took up the mythologem after it had lain motionless for many years and gave it new movement and life. This is the case with the poets of modern times. Myths became a part of their own experience and thus they were enabled to communicate a *peira* of their own, and not a mere knowledge of the material, not a mere orientation based on their studies and mode of culture, but a true *peira*. Both categories of poets enhance the resonance that the content awakens in us.

[5

T H E theme of Prometheus has repeatedly been taken up by poets of modern times, whose imaginations have been fired by the *Prometheus Bound,* the only part of the Aischylean trilogy to have come down to us in its entirety. Readers of English have the great advantage of a poetic rendering of the *Prometheus Bound* by Elizabeth Barrett Browning. In his lyrical drama *Prometheus Unbound,* Shelley attempted to fill in the gap created by the loss of Aischylos' tragedy of the same name, but took an entirely new view of the theme. Quite unlike Goethe, he possessed a thorough knowledge of the Greek poets; it was quite intentionally that he deviated from the conception of Aischylos and created a completely modern work. Of this work it has rightly been said that in it "lies the quintessence of all Shelley's subtlety," [11] and that it "echoes again and again with all the best scientific knowledge of Shelley's generation." [12] What Shelley refashions is not the mythologem of Prometheus but the prophecy concerning the liberation of Prometheus, which he develops into a poem on the future of mankind. He speaks far more like a prophet than like the ancient *mythológoi*, for he relates not what originally was but what will be.

Goethe is no less a modern man than Shelley. As a man, he is closer to us than the ancient myth makers are. But he took over what they had done and so became a modern *mythológos*. He knew far less Greek than Shelley, and this helped him to treat the ancient material with greater freedom. To a certain degree, Shelley carried on the Greek tradition like a Hellenistic poet, and that is just what Goethe did not do; he was more primitive. Here we shall consider his Prometheus poems not merely from the standpoint of literary criticism but also on the basis of mythological science. He stands, as it were, halfway between us and antiquity. This he does in two respects. For one thing he communicates a *peira* of the human substance; for another his new mythologem can create an obstacle to our understanding of the old mythologem. On the other hand, he helps us by interpreting his own work in a way paralleled by no other modern poet.

After all, our study of a mythologem cannot begin where the

---

11. Neville Rogers, *Shelley at Work*, p. 16.
12. Newman Ivey White, *Shelley*, II, 129.

mythologem began. It is a paradox of mythology that the mythologems —that is, the broad lines of early versions of myths—and the characters in the drama are already historically present wherever we choose to begin. Ingenious as they may be, hypotheses concerning origins—most of them are the products of indemonstrable theories devised by modern men—can only lead us away from the field of serious scientific endeavor. Not so an interpretation that the reader can examine in the text. Since, as we have said, Goethe, of all the mythologists who have dealt with this material, stands closest to us and gives us an interpretation of his own ideas, we choose to approach the mythologem through his work—the lyric poem *Prometheus* and the fragments of his Prometheus play.

C. K.

Ascona, Switzerland

Summer, 1962

Acknowledgment is gratefully made to W. W. Norton & Co. for quotations from Edith Hamilton's translation of *Prometheus Bound* in *Three Greek Plays,* and to the University of Chicago Press for a quotation from Richmond Lattimore's translation of the *Odes of Pindar,* copyright 1947 by The University of Chicago.

PROMETHEUS:

Archetypal Image of Human Existence

I. WHO IS GOETHE'S PROMETHEUS?

Prometheus and Christ

AMONG ALL the gods of Greece, it is Prometheus who stands in the most remarkable relation to mankind. He presents a striking resemblance and a striking contrast to the Christian Saviour. More than any other Greek god, he intercedes for mankind, makes common cause with men. Therein lies the resemblance. But Christ suffered human existence as a man. His whole mission depended on his close bond with mankind. The paradox in his case is not that he, a man, made common cause with mankind. The paradox is the faith of the Christians who believe him to be a god. Prometheus never appears as a man. He is a mythological being and was never anything else; it is not as though a mythology had formed round him later on. His divinity is self-evident. In his case, the paradox begins when he defends the cause of humanity, when he, a god, suffers injustice, torment, and humiliation—the hallmarks of human existence. The paradox is precisely his bond with mankind. Just as the divinity of Christ is an intrinsic part of the Christian faith, so Prometheus' bond with mankind is an intrinsic part of the Greek view of the world.

The only really comparable god might be the Gnostic Anthropos, "Man," or "Primordial Man," though here again there are important differences. However, a study of the Gnostic primordial man would take us into a very different field; we should be leaving mythology for Gnosis.[1] And in the present investigation we mean to confine ourselves

---

1. See Kerényi, "Mythologie und Gnosis," *EJ 1940/41* (VIII), pp. 157 ff.; in Albae Vigiliae (XIV), 1942.

to the mythological tradition, to disregard our own conceptions of divine redeemers and rebels, formed by Christianity and Gnosis, and set ourselves back into a state of not-yet-knowing.

Such a state of innocence is not to be achieved at one stroke. It is not enough to say: forget all about Goethe's *Prometheus*. Obviously, those who are not acquainted with it will not think of it at all. But many others have experienced Prometheus through it. The question is only: which Prometheus? one who has nothing to do with the Prometheus recorded by ancient poets and modern scholars? A critic of Goethe's works on Prometheus advises us to forget all about Greek mythology in approaching them.[2] That is easily said. But it is not easy to forget either the Greeks or Goethe. Goethe has provided us, in the form of a monologue, with a kind of preface to any serious study of the Prometheus theme.

The 'Prometheus' of Goethe[3]

> *Cover your heavens, O Zeus,*
> *With cloudy mist*
> *And like a little boy*
> *Cutting the heads off thistles,*
> *Practice your hand*
> *On oak trees and mountain peaks;*
> *But you will have to let*
> *My earth stand*
> *And my hut that you did not build,*
> *And my hearth*
> *For whose fire*
> *You envy me.*

2. Emil Staiger, *Goethe*, 1749–1786. His interpretation of the Prometheus poems was published after the appearance of the first version of the present study in Albae Vigiliae (N. S. IV, Zurich, 1946), and is here critically discussed without further references.   3. *Werke* (ed. Beutler), I, 320 f.; tr. R. M.

I know of nothing poorer
Under the sun than you gods.
Wretchedly
You feed your majesty
On imposed sacrifices
And the breath of prayers.
You would waste away
If children and beggars
Were not hopeful fools.

When I was a child,
Hopelessly perplexed,
I turned my confused eye
To the sun, as though it had
An ear to hear my plaint,
A heart like mine,
To take pity on one oppressed.

Who helped me
Against the pride of the Titans?
Who saved me from death
And slavery?
Did you not do it all alone,
O ardent, holy heart?
And young and good,
Cheated, did you not shine
A message of thanksgiving
Upon the sleeper up there?

I honor you? What for?
Did you ever appease the pain
Of the sufferer?
Did you ever quench the tears
Of the fearful?

Was I not forged into a man
By all-powerful time
And eternal fate,
My masters and yours?
Did you suppose
I should hate life,
Flee to the desert
Because not all
My dream flowers bore fruit?

Here I sit, shaping man
After my image,
A race that is like me,
To suffer, to weep,
To rejoice and be glad,
And like myself
To have no regard for you!

The Dramatic Fragment

I N the foregoing poem, Goethe put his very own thoughts, the product of intense experience, into the traditional mythological figure. Did he do so without preparation? or was the dramatic fragment on Prometheus already in existence, and did his work on the "drama" (letter to Kestner, July, 1773 [4]) bring forth such fruit? The question has recently been revived and incorrectly answered by a number of prominent Goethe critics.[5] Thus we cannot content ourselves with the impression that with the almost unparalleled violence of these stanzas

4. Ibid., XVIII, 201.
5. This is not the case with Humphry Trevelyan, *Goethe and the Greeks*, p. 62.

Goethe burst the framework of the play which he had already begun. When the dramatic fragment,[6] lost for nearly half a century, reappeared, Goethe stated quite clearly that the "monologue in question" had been intended to open the third act (letter to Zelter, May 11, 1820[7]). Accordingly, when the recovered two acts were published in 1830, he inserted the monologue after them with the stage direction: "Prometheus in his workshop." The passages in which the dramatic fragment complements and wholly fits in with the poem bear witness to the excellence of Goethe's memory and enable us to follow the young *mythológos* in him—for in those days he was far more of a modern *mythológos* than a playwright.

In the monologue Goethe speaks of "my earth":

> *But you will have to let*
> *My earth stand . . .*

Does this "my" mean possession or familiarity, does it suggest a bond with the earth or a sense of belonging to it? Though everything else stands out more clearly in the monologue than in the preceding two acts of the play, it is the dramatic fragment we must consult if we wish to measure the precise weight of this word and clearly discern the cosmogonic situation. The world was to be divided. The gods were willing to leave Olympos to Prometheus and keep only the heavens for themselves: up there on Olympos—this is the suggestion that his brother Epimetheus brings from the gods—

> *shall you live*
> *And rule the earth.*

---

6. Goethe, *Werke* (ed. Beutler), IV, 185–97; the passages quoted (tr. R. M.) are from pp. 186–90.   7. Ibid., XXI, 392.

But Prometheus declares that he already *has* the earth, not because it is allotted to him like a piece of property but because it belongs to him naturally:

> *What I have they cannot rob me of,*
> *And as for what they have let them defend it.*
> *Here mine and there thine,*
> *Thus are we separate.*

BROTHER: *How much then is yours?*

PROMETHEUS: *The realm occupied by my action.*
Nothing below and nothing above it.
What right over me
Have those stars up there
That they should gape at me?

For the young *mythológos*, Prometheus is "Lord of the Earth"—just as Hades is "Lord of the Underworld"—in a special, mythological sense, on the strength of an initial division, and not because he created it, for he did not. The notion that the "work of each day," of which Prometheus speaks, should be taken in a Biblical sense as the work of Creation, is surely erroneous. And in Goethe's mythologem Prometheus' work of creation is indeed limited exclusively to what he can create on the earth.

> *Here is my world, my universe.*
> *Here is where I feel myself to be.*
> *Here are all my desires*
> *In bodily form.*
> *My spirit divided a thousandfold*
> *And whole in my beloved children.*

In the beginning it was only

> *His world of clay*

and then, by the life-giving power of Fate, it came alive:

> *Look down, O Zeus,*
> *Upon my world: it lives.*

The Lord of the Earth, whose spirit is divided a thousandfold in his creatures, men, does not look upon himself as a god, for he leaves this name to those in heaven, but he knows that he is just as eternal and omnipotent as they, thanks to the power which is inherent in his spirit and which the gods, lords of the powers of nature, do not possess:

> *Can you gather the broad*
> *Spaces of heaven and earth*
> *Into my hand for me?*

—for that the creative artist can do.

> *Can you divide me*
> *From myself?*

—for the poet can do that.

> *Can you stretch me,*
> *Can you expand me into a world?*

For that man as such can do by virtue of his spirit. The gods have the power. Another power is opposed to them: the power of the spirit which knows itself not as itself but as a divinity, namely, as Minerva (as it was then customary to call Pallas Athene). That is the clear meaning of the dialogue with the goddess:

PROMETHEUS: *Those were thy words.*
Then I was not myself,
And a god spoke
When I thought to speak.
And when I thought a god spoke
I myself spoke.
So was it between thee and me
So fervently one.
Eternal is my love for thee.

But the gods cannot give life or take it away, nor can the Lord of the Earth—or by now we may call him "Man"—do so by the power of his divine spirit. This only Fate can do, as Prometheus learns from the goddess at the end of the first act when, by the life-giving power of Fate, the "source of all life" is revealed. The second act is devoted to life with a fervor that Nietzsche could not have surpassed. This act explains Prometheus' now boundless love of further creation with which the third act begins. We have already entered into the second with the quotation:

Look down, O Zeus,
Upon my world: it lives.

And the speech continues:

I have shaped it in my image,
A race like unto me.
To suffer, to weep, to enjoy and be glad,
And like myself to have no regard for you

—lines that recur in the monologue. Goethe would not have written them down in this way if they had already been present in the finer form already known to us. Here they are still unpolished, in their original state.

Comparison of a further sequence of almost identical lines in the dialogue with Mercury and in the monologue shows not only greater polish in the latter but also a sharper delineation of the childhood mythologem. We learn from the dramatic fragment that Goethe's Prometheus had Zeus for father and a goddess for mother. With this change from the traditional lineage the poet distinguished his hero from the race of the Titans. He also set him in conflict with them, by giving an intimation of dangers to which the boy or youth was exposed. Mercury reproaches him with lack of gratitude toward his parents who protected him.

PROMETHEUS: *From what! From dangers*
That they feared!
Did they protect my heart
From serpents that secretly tormented it!
Did they steel my breast
To defy the Titans?

In all probability the mythologem Goethe had in mind is an incident in the childhood of Zeus' son Herakles, who was saved from the menacing snakes not by his father but by himself. It is left uncertain whether Prometheus had to do with real or with psychic monsters. In the monologue there is a more distinct allusion to another son of Zeus, Dionysos, who was torn to pieces by the Titans or (in the Homeric hymn [8]) delivered into slavery:

8. The seventh (ed. Allen).

> *Who helped me*
> *Against the pride of the Titans?*
> *Who saved me from death*
> *And slavery?*

The fragment continues:

> *Was I not forged into a man*
> *By all-powerful Time,*
> *My Lord and yours?*

Nor is Fate, whose life-giving power Prometheus learns of at the end of the second act, forgotten in the monologue:

> *Was I not forged into a man*
> *By all-powerful Time*
> *And eternal Fate,*
> *My masters and yours?*

Goethe Interprets His Mythologem

I N 1813 or 1814, in the first period of his writing of *Dichtung und Wahrheit*,[9] Goethe undertook, toward the end of Book XV, to explain the Prometheus fragments. It seems unlikely that he had forgotten the dramatic fragments which at that time were lost. The second sentence of his explanation mentions the "protection of parents and relatives," and Mercury also speaks of it in the first lines of the unfinished drama:

> *And protected thee!*

The interpretation begins significantly with the first sentence: "The common fate of man, which all of us have to bear, | must weigh most

9. *Poetry and Truth from My Own Life* (tr. Minna Steele Smith), II, 177 ff.

heavily on those whose intellectual powers expand early and rapidly." [10] I have inserted a dividing line between the two elements which Goethe himself stressed at the outset as the most important for an understanding of his Prometheus mythologem: on the one hand, the common fate of men and, on the other, the more intelligent man who suffers more from it than others.

The youthful Goethe, evoked forty-two years later in *Dichtung und Wahrheit,* had experienced both elements—the human lot and the fact that it is almost unendurable for the exceptional man. In retrospect he sees himself "treading the wine-press alone": a figure taken from Isaiah 63:3 [11] which at the same time recalls an occupation of the primordial men in Goethe's Prometheus play of 1807–8, the *Pandora:* [12]

> *All the vintners coming forth*
> *From the wine-presses, the cliff cellars. . . .*

In this primordial situation, which each man experiences for himself, in essential solitude, as though he were God, he had to establish the foundations of an "existence." Goethe utters the word and speaks of what made it possible for him to establish an existence at that time, namely, his productive talent: "I liked in thought to base my whole existence upon it. This conception soon assumed a distinct form, the old mythological image of Prometheus . . . who, apart from the gods, peopled a world from his own workshop." [13]

10. Ibid., II, 177.
11. This was pointed out to me by Professor B. B. Kurzweil, Bar-Ilan University, Ramat Gan, Israel.
12. In *Werke* (ed. Beutler), VI, 406–43; the passage that we quote (tr. R. M.) is from p. 441.
13. *Poetry and Truth* (tr. Smith), p. 178.

Goethe's mythologem is not concerned with human existence in general and its founding. Nor with art and its invention or introduction for the purpose of softening human existence: this, too, like the heaviness of the human lot, Goethe had experienced in himself. This was the *other* fact, side by side with the common fate of men, upon which the poet wished to build his own individual existence. And so he thought of Prometheus, a particular sort of being between the gods and the Titans. Indeed, he describes his mythological method in some detail and clearly designates two elements: "The fable of Prometheus came alive in me. I cut the old Titan robe to my own size. . . ." [14] Prometheus is not the artist in general but Goethe as a young man: hence the lyrical character of what sprang from this mythologizing. But mythologizing it remained. The two characteristic elements of this occupation are indicated: the spontaneity with which a mythological figure and its story—a mythologem—seek expression as individual experience, and the search for expression in the mythological tradition.

In this, however, Goethe was freer than the old *mythológos*. He himself says that he cut the garment of the Titan to his own size. But his method strongly suggests the way in which I myself, following Mann and Ortega, have described the mythological attitude in speaking of peoples with a still living mythology; [15] archaic man, before doing anything, stepped back a pace like a bullfighter poising himself for the death stroke. He sought an example in the past, and into it he slipped as into a diving bell, in order to plunge, at once protected and distorted, into the problems of the present.

Goethe's problem at the time, according to his own statement, was

14. Goethe, *Werke* (ed. Beutler), X, 699.
15. Cf. the Introduction, p. xvi.

the grounding of his *individual existence,* something far more existential than any general theorizing about art and artists. In attempting to solve the problem of his own life by identifying himself with a mythological figure, he created a mythologem, and proceeded more in the manner of a *mythológos* than of a dramatist. But in holding fast to his own particular experience, that of his isolation, and slipping into the poetic expression of this state, the monologue, he not only burst out of the dramatic form that his material might still have permitted but broke with the mythological tradition as well—and fell back into the original mythologem, which he enriched with a trait that was new but that he discerned in the ancient image of Prometheus.

The Modern Element in Goethe's Mythologem

T H E modern trait that stands out clearly in Goethe's experience at that time is the isolation of every man, a lot which the poet resolutely accepted. In his interpretation, he speaks, in the light of his mature wisdom, of this isolation and of the consequences of his acceptance of it. "My works that had met with so much approval were children of solitude and after my relation to the world had broadened, there was no lack of inventive power and enthusiasm, but the execution faltered, for I had no real style either in prose or in verse, and in each new piece of work, according to the nature of the subject, I had to grope forward and make new experiments. Since in this I had to reject, to exclude the help of men, I cut myself off, *like Prometheus, from the gods as well,* and this was all the more natural because, in view of my character and manner of thinking, one attitude always engulfed and repelled all others." [16]

A consequence of this affirmation of human existence, including its isolation, and of the break with the gods it implies, was Goethe's Prometheus mythologem. His Prometheus was similar to the ancient god who went his own way by espousing the cause of men, and yet he did not resemble the true "gigantic, heaven-storming" Titans. This Prometheus only wished to isolate himself, and for this very reason he did not want to be a god but, like the young Goethe, wanted to found a "third dynasty"—mankind. Yet how could the founder remain isolated if with him mankind embarked on the common fate—isolation? But had this isolation not, from time immemorial, been a trait of human beings, which came to be known only now, so that precisely this new Prometheus was the genuine one, and his mythologem the true mythologem of the human lot—seen from the standpoint of the modern era? A far more complicated mythologem than the ancient one, but still the result of a mythological occupation continuing the old one.

One implication of all this was that Goethe saw the boy Prometheus in the situation of the primordial orphan child of the original mythologem: that is, in the manner of the ancient mythological tales which, in their images, directly reflect the condition into which every mortal is born. [17] Whether he was actually thinking of Herakles menaced by the serpents or of the child Dionysos dismembered by the Titans need not be decided. The Prometheus assailed by the Titans is no longer Greek mythology but a mythology created by Goethe. And it is typical

16. Goethe, *Werke* (ed. Beutler), X, 698 f.
17. Kerényi, "The Primordial Child in Primordial Times."

of his mythologizing that, of all the traditions concerning Prometheus, he chose to adopt a pictorial one based on a drawing after the Roman sarcophagus relief in Montfaucon:[18] There sits Prometheus, forming the image of a man, beside him a basket of clay, before him a finished figure receiving from Minerva a soul in the form of a butterfly [I, IIa].

Can we, indeed need we, supply an answer to the question of who Goethe's Prometheus is, if neither a god, a Titan, nor a man? Whether intentionally or unintentionally, his manner of creating man is Biblical; his emphatic contempt for God is in like degree anti-Biblical: that was the impression it was bound to arouse, and essentially this hostility to God seems to have been a different kind of dependence on the Bible. This role as a creator hostile to God defines Goethe's Prometheus. A poetic "middle figure," says Goethe in his interpretation, minimizing his significance and excluding any idea that mythologizing might not be a merely poetic occupation but carry a peculiar responsibility, although he does not pass over in silence the death of the pious Moses Mendelssohn, who died of his encounter with this new Prometheus. Goethe's Prometheus is no God, no Titan, no man, but the immortal prototype of man as the original rebel and affirmer of his fate: the original inhabitant of the earth, seen as an antigod, as Lord of the Earth. In this connection he seems more Gnostic than Greek, but he surely is in no way related to the childlike Gnosis of Goethe when he was still younger. He belongs rather to the more recent history of ideas and anticipates the Nietzschean or Existentialist view of man. Or perhaps he goes even further. Young

18. *L'Antiquité expliquée et representée en figures* (Paris, 1719), I, pt. 1, pl. fol. p. 24. Described also in Hederich's *Reales Schullexicon*, p. 2329; cf. Goethe's *Werke* (ed. Beutler), IV, 1038.

Goethe's mythologizing could not resurrect the classical figure of Prometheus, but inevitably gave rise to a thoroughly modern one, whose effect on the younger generation was greatly feared by the old master at the time when the lost pages reappeared (letter to Zelter, May 11, 1820 [19]).

---

19. Goethe, *Werke* (ed. Beutler), XXI, 392.

II. THE TITANIC, AND THE ETERNITY OF THE HUMAN RACE

The Human Race and the Races of Men

ISOLATION as a *common* fate—this modern contradiction—was not part of the Greek image of man. In the eyes of the Greeks, humanity was distinguished from divinity with all possible clarity: it was at once *deilón* and *deinón*.[1] There was nothing poorer, more insignificant, more tormented in their eyes, than the lot of man. And yet there was ground enough for the words of the chorus in the *Antigone* of Sophokles:

> *Terrible are many things*
> *but nothing more terrible than man.*[2]

Thus was the human race conceived over against the race of the "lightly living gods." Hesiod, surely on the basis of oriental models, told of whole races of men that had died out,[3] and up to the end of antiquity men believed it necessary to celebrate certain festivals, such as the Eleusinian Mysteries, in order that the whole human race should not vanish.[4] The doom of mankind was expected of Neptunian or Vulcanic natural catastrophes—to use Goethe's terms—or from famine, war, or periodic upheavals. The death of the individual was no threat to the human race; the mortality of mortals was just one

---

1. "Der Mensch in griechischer Anschauung," in Kerényi, *Niobe,* pp. 240 ff. The *deilón* is the wretched, the *deinón* the terrible and prodigious.
2. 332–34 (cf. LCL edn., I, 340).
3. *Works and Days* 106–201. On Hesiod's oriental models: R. Reitzenstein and H. H. Schäder, *Studien zum antiken Synkretismus.*
4. Cf. my *Die Mysterien von Eleusis.*

shading—the darkest of all—in the comprehensive attribute of *deilón,* the general human wretchedness. A view of the eternity of the human race detached itself from the dark images of the future set forth in certain prophecies, but it was not incompatible with a recognition of the power of the gods of death. Let us consider this view.

A Pythagorean Doctrine

Illa sententia, qua semper humanum genus fuisse creditur, auctores habet Pythagoram Samium et Ocellum Lucanum et Archytam Tarentinum omnesque adeo Pythagoricos: According to these words of the Late Roman author Censorinus, in his book *On Birthdays,*[5] Pythagoras of Samos, Okellos of Lukania, Archytas of Tarentum, and in general all Pythagoreans were the authors and proponents of the opinion that the human race was eternal. The Pythagorean view of the matter is known to us from the work *On the Cosmos* bearing the name of Okellos. Somewhat freely translated, it runs as follows:

"Man arose neither from earth nor from other living things, animals or plants. For if we assume the cosmic order to be eternal, without beginning and without end—and that is the thesis of the Pythagoreans—then the whole, whose order (*diakósmēsis*) is the world order (*kósmos*), must likewise be eternal. In the first place, the parts of this eternal whole must always have existed: the heavens, the earth, and between them the air, since without them there can be no world, for the world after all consists of them. And if the parts are eternal, then everything they contain must also have existed from all time: in the sky the sun, the moon, and the stars, in the earth the

5. *De die natali* IV 3.

animals and plants, gold and silver, in the air the winds and the changes of temperature. For the sky is sky precisely because it contains these things, and for like reason is the earth earth and the air air. And now, since to each one of these parts a race is assigned that stands over everything else it contains—to the heavens the gods, to the earth men, to the sphere of the air the daemons—the human race must necessarily be eternal: that is, if we are right in assuming that not only the parts are coexistent with the cosmos—the order—but also that which is contained in the parts, namely, that which is ordered." [6]

Here, in a work written before the first century B.C., the Greek idea of the cosmos as *diakósmēsis*, of the world as order, is developed to its ultimate consequences. It is evident that this conception includes the idea that the human race is eternal, even though it does not, as in a naïvely anthropocentric cosmology, stand in the center, or even, as might be the case in a less naïve philosophical reflection, if man is not construed as the orderer of this order or as one orderer among several. The naïve, prephilosophical view of the world, the result not of philosophizing but of mythologizing, which underlies all this, does not have man as its center. It has two poles, man on earth, the gods in heaven. Merely for the sake of symmetry, as it were, the daemons— not evil spirits but beings intermediate between God and man—occupy a middle position in the air, the realm between heaven and earth. They were not a product of Greek mythology, but of the belief in daemons that had sprung up in various parts of the Mediterranean world and the Near East.

---

6. III 1–3 (cf. edn. and tr. into German by Rotermund, pp. 24–25).

The World View of Greek Mythology

T H E duality of gods and men, two races standing in polar opposition, is expressed so clearly in some of the older poets that we may recognize it as a basic trait of the Greek mythological world view:

> *There is one*
> *race of men, one race of gods; both have breath*
> *of life from a single mother. But sundered power*
> *holds us divided, so that one side is nothing, while on the*
> *   other the brazen sky is established*
> *a sure citadel forever.*[7]

Thus, in the sixth Nemean Ode, Pindar joins and separates the races of men and the gods. The division is absolute. On the one side, men: they are nothing. On the other, heaven eternal and unshakable, the abode of the gods. Eternal freedom from danger is here an attribute of the abode of the gods, the sky, which surrounds the human race as though with its body; but it is also a characteristic of those who dwell on high, whom the sky serves as a throne. By virtue of this attribute, the surrounding element, the sky, coincides with the gods, the other race, which delimits the human race. And yet this surrounding, delimiting element is not really corporeal—that is, tangible—for man, but intangible and yet hard: "brazen." Here the metal does not express any supposed materiality, or anything that can be visu-

7. Pindar, Nemean Ode VI (cf. tr. Lattimore, p. 111).

> ἓν ἀνδρῶν
> ἓν θεῶν γένος· ἐκ μιᾶς δὲ πνέομεν
> ματρὸς ἀμφότεροι, διείργει δὲ πᾶσα κεκριμένα
> δύναμις ὡς τὸ μὲν οὐδέν, ὁ δὲ χάλκεος ἀσφαλὲς αἰὲν ἕδος
> μένει οὐρανός.

alized in connection with the sky, but something paradoxical: the incomprehensible hardness of something intangible—the gods and their abode.

Pindar, however, not only divides but also unites the gods and men. Hesiod had done so before him in his *Works and Days* (108): he will sum up, he says, "how the gods and mortal men sprang from one source." [8]

To the minds of both poets, this is something that must never be forgotten, not even when they speak of the decline or the insignificance of the human race. According to the great mythological tradition of the Greeks, man as well as the gods is descended from Gaia, the Earth Mother. In this mythological world based on the earth and divided into gods and men, there is no suggestion of a creation of man. Man is represented neither as a creation nor as a rebel, but as one pole of the cosmos, the other being the heavenly gods.

Who Were the Titans?

T H E S E basic traits of the Greek mythological world view which, like the Prometheus of the young Goethe, stand here as a motto and preamble have made something clear to us. And at the same time they have raised a question. They have made it clear, as already intimated, that Hesiod and Aischylos, our sources for the Prometheus mythologem of the archaic and the early classical periods, are far removed from any notion that man was created by the Titan. For the mythologi-

8. All Hesiod quotations, with the exception of those on our pp. 45 and 47, are from Evelyn-White's translation. Here, his pp. 10–11.

ὡς ὁμόθεν γεγάασι θεοὶ θνητοί τ' ἄνθρωποι.

cal view of the world, like the figures of mythology, has this paradoxical trait: it was there before the poets, yet it is the poets who give it form. In interpreting the classical texts on Prometheus, we shall have to forget all about his creation of man. The question that has been raised is this: how could a cosmology include such beings as the Titans if they were neither gods nor men nor something in between after the manner of the daemons?

And so, even at the risk of anticipating some of our story, we must, before beginning to interpret the myth, reply to the question "Who were the Titans?" The texts provide an answer that speaks pretty much for itself. Of course we should know more about the Titans if the epic poem *Titanomachia*, the War of the Titans, which tradition attributes to Eumelos of Corinth, or to Arkinos of Miletos, or to another post-Homeric poet, had been preserved. Works of archaic literature, mythological epics, take on a particular importance in this connection because most of the Titans had no cult in Greece. Hesiod shows us that the Greek narratives of the gods were influenced by such poems, particularly by a work that had become almost canonical, and he also shows us the limits of such influence. I say "almost," because after all there were limits to the acceptance and influence of such poems, and I say "canonical" to indicate that a work of this kind cannot have been a free poetic invention—that would have been impossible both for chronological and for material reasons—but must have been a poetic treatment of a *tradition* and as such subject to certain restrictions, even if the tradition was oriental rather than Greek in origin. Successful poets "canonize," that is, they endow certain narratives with a special importance and influence; but they cannot "canonize" a tale that is generally regarded as their own invention. Anyone who chooses to find in this material purely poetic inventions or innovations such as are customary in modern poetry must in every instance supply special proofs.[9]

Hesiod discloses a limit to the influence of the *Titanomachia* upon Greek mythology by this failure to accept the archaic genealogy of Uranos (which never gained universal Greek acceptance), namely, the descent of the god "Heaven" from a celestial father (Aither, "Light of Heaven," according to the *Titanomachia*, or Akmon, "Anvil," according to an unknown ancient source). After Hesiod, who next to Homer was the most successful "canonizer" among Greek poets, such a change in the genealogy of the gods would scarcely have been conceivable. Hesiod was able to express the mythological world view of the Greeks by way of genealogy.[10] The answer of his *Theogony* to our question is this: the Titans were gods, the earlier gods, *próteroi theoí* (424). Gaia, the Earth, the Pristine Mother, had borne them by Uranos, her firstborn son. As gods and sons of Heaven, they belonged to the divine-heavenly pole of the two-part cosmology. But nearly all of them ended up under ground, in the deepest maw of the earth, under Tartaros, where no cult could reach them. They bear—even proleptically, in anticipation of their subsequent fate (697)—the epithet *chthónioi*, the "subterranean"; otherwise they are called *hypotartárioi*, "subtartarean" (851), in agreement with the Iliad (XIV 279) and also substantially with the Homeric hymn to Apollo (335). When they broke loose, as when they appeared to slay the child Dionysos in the Orphic poem of Onomakritos,[11] a theologian of the sixth century, they

9. This was not done, for example, by Karl Reinhardt, who wished to ascribe so essential a trait in the tradition as the Titanic origin of Prometheus to the poetic invention or innovation of Aischylos and waged what strikes us as a strange "Titanomachia" against the *Titanomachia*, which *could* certainly have contained this trait. See his *Aischylos als Regisseur und Theologe*, p. 30.

10. Paula Philippson, *Untersuchungen über griechischen Mythos: Genealogie als mythische Form*.

11. Pausanias III 37 5; Onomakritos in O. Kern, *Orphicorum fragmenta*, p. 56.

joined with the daemons to whom the Pythagoreans assigned the middle zone.

But not all of them ended in this way: above all, not their sisters, the great daughters of Heaven. Hesiod, and perhaps also the *Titanomachia*, made them, like the Titans, six in number in order to complete the celestial number twelve. The tradition does not tell us whether they took part in the battle of the Titans, or if so, which of them. The battle and the defeat of the Titans account for the strange polarity "son-of-Heaven–subterranean" that is characteristic of the Titans. Where polarity is replaced by periodicity, as in the case of Phoibe, whose name assuredly means "moon goddess," there was no need for a battle or defeat. The names Titan and Titanis, "Titaness," imply more than merely gods who were defeated by other gods. In this view of the world, the others, "those descended from Kronos" (*Theogony* 630 and elsewhere)—Zeus, his brothers, sisters, and children—are only the dominant minority, a segment as it were of the "brazen sky," which includes so visible a Titan as the sun [12] and so visible a Titaness as the moon.[13]

The Titans were by no means limited to a single generation of "earlier gods." *Próteroi theoí* may be understood more accurately to mean "those who were gods even earlier" than Zeus and his Olympian family. Most of them waged war against Zeus and his followers and were defeated; others, like Okeanos and Tethys, retained their rank and functions; still others were perpetuated in their descendants as were Hyperion and Theia, the most notable couple among the Titans, in Helios and Selene, Sun and Moon. In Hesiod, descent expressed

12. Empedokles, in Diels, fr. 38 (an English version in K. Freeman, *Ancilla to the Pre-Socratic Philosophers*, p. 57).
13. Apollonios Rhodios, *Argonautica* IV 54 (cf. LCL edn., p. 299).

kindred essence. In the *Theogony*, the essential kinship—in this case, kinship in Titanism—between Iapetos, the Titan with the strange name, and his descendants is characterized in part by the presence among the sons of Iapetos of the less known Menoitios along with Atlas, Prometheus, and Epimetheus (510). Menoitios is an exemplary representative of Titanism (quite apart from the fact that he is not a son but a grandson of Heaven); he is also depicted as such and suffers the fate of most of the Titans: Zeus with his thunderbolt dashes him, the *hybristḗs*, into *érebos*, the eternal darkness of the underworld (514–16), because of his *atasthalíē* and exuberant virility (*ēnoréē hypéroplos*).

What Did 'Titanic' Mean to the Greeks?

Hybristḗs and *atasthalíē* are difficult words to translate, but their meaning is clear. They go together (Iliad XIII 633–34). They designate unlimited, violent insolence, particularly that of the Titans. In one passage of the *Theogony* (209), where Hesiod specifically imputes *atasthalíē* to the Titans, he sees himself obliged to explain the name Titan by an etymological artifice, because for the Greeks it was by no means clear and self-evident. We have the same situation as in the Odyssey (XIX 406), where Autolykos, the grandfather, is introduced in order that he may give his grandson the name of Odysseus. From the standpoint of the Homeric and post-Homeric language this name is only seemingly clear, and Autolykos tries, with the arts of popular etymology—as this incorrect method is called today—to explain what is seemingly self-evident. It is Uranos, the father, who gives the Titans

their name, and his etymologies—from *titaínein*, to exert, and *tísis*—
the "retribution" meted out to the "exertion" of the Titans—are false.
Even so, they characterize Titanism as known to the Greeks at Hesiod's
time. Thus our introductory question "Who were the Titans?" must be
answered in the light of another question: "What did the Greeks mean
by Titanic?"

Hýbris and *atasthalíē*, boundless pride and violence, or however
we wish to translate them, were not qualities limited to the Titans, nor
was their "exuberant virility"—on the basis of which (and of the false
etymology from *titaínein*) they were regarded in late antiquity as
Priapic gods. The two words related phonetically to "Titan" that have
come down to us, *títax* and *titḗnē*, also required explanation for
the Greek readers of the poetic texts in which they occurred: they
were explained respectively as "king" and "queen"—meanings not
incompatible with the interpretations "earlier gods" and sons of
Heaven. Since names of gods belonging to the victorious Olympian
family are to be found in documents of the Mycenaean—or in Crete
the late Minoan—period, it is no longer possible to say that the Titans
were simply their predecessors in the cult and that their defeat, which
characterizes all known histories of the Titans, is a mythological expression for historic changes of religion. "There are many indications,"
writes Walter F. Otto,[14] "that [the name Titan] acquired the con-
notation of 'wild,' 'rebellious,' or even 'wicked' by opposition to the
Olympians, to whom the Titans yielded only after a struggle." Precisely
of this there is no evidence whatever. It is more likely that the cult of
Pallas Athene and Hera—two great goddesses under the rule of Zeus—
went back to the Bronze Age [15] or even to the neolithic era.[16] On the

---

14. *The Homeric Gods*, p. 33.
15. Kerényi, *Die Jungfrau und Mutter der griechischen Religion.*
16. Kerényi, "Zeus und Hera," *Saeculum*, I (1950), 250.

other hand, the Mycenaean documents of Pylos attest the cult of at least one of the Titanesses, in the *Theia mater*, whom Pindar still glorified eight hundred years later.[17]

We have already noted the strangeness of the name Iapetos. He and Kronos—another name that our present knowledge of Greek does not clarify—appear in the Iliad (VIII 479) as the two great examples which sufficed to call forth the mythologem of the Titans. Here there is nothing to suggest any cult of the Titans or change of cult in Greece itself, but a number of indications point to a mythology with a historic background embracing several nations and empires.[18] The gods of Asia Minor disclose vast historic changes corresponding to radical ethnic changes on earth. Tales about battles of the gods in the polyglot Hittite empire, fragmentary texts containing names of gods with diverse linguistic origins, show points of contact with the Greek tales of the Titans. However, they are worlds apart from the basic features and the central motif of Hesiod's version—the will of the all-bearing mother earth.[19] There is a Hittite dethronement mythologem limited to male deities and running through four generations of gods. In it the god corresponding to the Greek Uranos has a male predecessor: a feature rejected by Hesiod, but accepted by the *Titanomachia*.[20] Here an extremely simplified history of the successive empires in the Near East prior to the first millennium B.C. had entered into mythology. Characterized by a masculine aggressiveness, it had become known to the Greeks through tales or even through epic songs.

In the Greek view, the mutual hostility of such rulers of heaven was

17. Pylos Fr 1202; Pindar, Isthmian Ode V 1 (ed. Bowra).
18. Kerényi, "Die Götter und die Weltgeschichte," in *Geistiger Weg Europas*, pp. 38–50.
19. W. F. Otto, "Der ursprüngliche Mythos," *EJ 1955* (XXIV), 326; Kerényi, "Dionysos und unsere Religionsgeschichte," *Wiener humanistische Blätter*, 1958, pp. 24–25, from 1951 lecture series.
20. J. Dörig in his Basel dissertation, *Der Kampf der Götter und Titanen*, p. 10.

"Titanic." From foreign mythologies the Greeks, made clear-sighted by their very strangeness, had derived the character which they associated with the non-Greek, but perhaps Mycenaean,[21] name of the Titans, and which they could also discern in ancient tales of their own showing the primordial characteristics of an archaic mythology superseded, though not entirely, by Homeric poetry. Among these characteristics was the identity of great divine figures with heavenly bodies—an identity which Homer no longer admitted, but which had its parallels in the Near East.

The Sufferings of Hera

A N D there is this too: the character of endangering and being endangered was not, in Greek mythologizing, limited to former fallen gods. The environing limit, the divine world itself, the heavens, otherwise so inflexible, proved in this respect to be strangely influenced by the human mode of existence. In concluding my preamble, starting from Goethe's Prometheus poems and reaching back, by way of the Pythagoreans, Pindar, and Hesiod to the mythological texts of the Hittites, I should like to recall a passage from Homer: "Hera suffered too, when the powerful Herakles, Amphitryon's son, struck her with a three-barbed arrow in the right breast—she had to bear incurable pain."[22]

With these words the goddess Dione comforted her daughter Aph-

21. Pylos Jn 04, 6. In 1951 Johannes Sundwall drew my attention to the Hittite hieroglyphic *titas*, "Father," after the reading of Gelb. Etymology from the Illyrian: Kretschmer, "Die protindogermanische Schicht," *Glotta*, XIV (1925), 309 f.
22. Iliad V 392–94 (tr. Rieu, p. 102, modified).

τλῆ δ' Ἥρη, ὅτε μιν κρατερὸς πάϊς Ἀμφιτρύωνος
δεξιτερὸν κατὰ μαζὸν ὀϊστῷ τριγλώχινι
βεβλήκει· τότε καί μιν ἀνήκεστον λάβεν ἄλγος.

rodite, who had been wounded by Diomedes. And then she went on to tell about the painful wound of Hades, king of the underworld, also inflicted by Herakles' arrow, and how it had been cured on Olympos by Paieon, the physician of the gods. Thus vulnerability was an attribute of the gods, just as it is characteristic of human existence.[23]

The difference between the two poles—the mortality of men and the immortality of gods—is immense. A god can wound and is vulnerable, he can cure and be cured; man can wound and be wounded; as a physician, he can heal and, considered as a wounded man, he can be healed. But considered as a man, he is incurable. Yet, strange to say, the lines we have quoted say something similar about Hera. The pain of the goddess is said to be "incurable."

Of course Homer and the post-Homeric poets took Hera's "incurable pain" not in a physical sense but rather as a sense of eternal injury. So Virgil in his high-sounding line:

> *Cum Iuno aeternum servans sub pectore vulnus*
> (*When Juno nursing an undying wound deep in her heart*).[24]

But it is certain that the poet to whom Homer's lines hark back did not take Hera's wound in this sense. The localization of the wound in the right breast and the lunar periodicity of the goddess's mythological joys and sufferings [25] show us that in this case the vulnerability of human existence has been extended to the cosmos, so that the periodic waning of the moon appears as a wound. From a nonmythological

---

23. Kerényi, *Asklepios*, pp. 77 and 79–82; and, on this battle of the gods, *The Heroes of the Greeks*, p. 165.
24. *Aeneid* I 36 (tr. Fairclough, I, 243).
25. Kerényi, *Tochter der Sonne*, p. 138, and *Saeculum*, I (1950), 248.

point of view, there would be no pain, and the word "incurable" would not apply:

> *Damna tamen celeres reparant caelestia lunae*
> (*Yet the swiftly changing moons repair their celestial*
>   *wounds*)

says Horace.[26] It is only from the human point of view that the wounds we see regularly renewed become incurable torment.

Thus no divine being is as close to human existence as the moonlike Hera. But does not Prometheus also bear a wound that is constantly renewed? He is the only Greek god who is in need of liberation and redemption from such a wound. Does this quality not create a profound bond between him and the still more unfortunate human race? This question, whose Greek implications we have yet to learn, does not necessarily point to a need of salvation in the Christian sense. However, it is a question that we shall do well to keep in mind as we make our way through the classical texts to this mysterious god of Greek mythology, wounded, in need of redemption, and also redeemed. First of all, we shall examine Hesiod's *Theogony,* then other archaic traditions and, after this preparation, the Prometheus tragedies of Aischylos.

26. *Odes* IV 7 13.

III. THE PROMETHEUS MYTHOLOGEM IN THE 'THEOGONY'

What Are Theogonies?

GREEK MYTHOLOGY knows of no creator of the world. Instead of creation myths, it contains theogonies, stories of the birth of the gods. Related successively, as in Hesiod's *Theogony*, they form whole series of epiphanies, in which the world appears in divine aspects, from which it is built up. The creator of a world is the poet. But this is creation only in an artistic sense. In so far as a creation of this sort *leads* to the building of a "world," in which men live as the Greeks lived in the Homeric and Hesiodic Zeus world, "establishment," or "founding" that brings a world into being, seems a much apter word than "creation." For the foundations of such a world lie not only in man, the creative being who makes it, but also in the harder, stronger matter from which the world is built and by virtue of which it is not a mere figment of thought but a subsisting "order." This order—which the Greeks called "cosmos"—was established by the unions and separations, the divine marriages and births, constituting a mythical history of the primordial beginnings which, taken as a whole, we call a "theogony."

The Marriage of Iapetos

ACCORDING to Hesiod's theogonic poem, the marriage of the Titan Iapetos formed part of the primordial sequence of unions and separations by which the rule of Zeus, as the Greek world order may be designated in mythological terms, was brought about. The name cannot be explained by any Greek etymology. As we have said, "Iapetos" sounds foreign (see p. 27). We first hear of him in Homer (Iliad VIII 478–81), where Zeus describes the place of extreme darkness to which Hera may retire in her anger if she pleases: ". . . you can go to the bottomless pit and join Iapetos and Kronos, who never enjoy the beams of Hyperion the Sun, nor any breezes, sunk as they are in the depths of Tartaros."[1]

It was thither that Zeus had banished the Titans after their defeat. But from both the Titans mentioned by Homer important lines were descended. That of Kronos leads upward to the eternal light of heaven, where Zeus and his children dwell. The line of Iapetos remains below, where it establishes temporal existence and determines the opposite pole from the celestial state: the fate of man.

At the beginning of this line stands the marriage of Iapetos, the union of a divine pair, from which Prometheus will be born (*Theogony* 507–12): "Now Iapetos took to wife the neat-ankled maid Klymene, daughter of Ocean, and went up with her into one bed. And she bare him a stouthearted son, Atlas: also she bare very glorious Menoitios and clever Prometheus, full of various wiles, and scatter-brained Epimetheus who from the first was a mischief to men who eat bread."[2]

According to this passage, the mother of Prometheus was a daughter of Okeanos, as were many of the great goddesses in Hesiod. Possibly she was the great mother of all the Titans, the Earth herself. In his *Prometheus Bound* (211–12),[3] Aischylos gives her the name of one of the Titanesses, Themis, who, however, should be taken as identical with Gaia. If we bear in mind that in one source the father of Prome-

1. Tr. Rieu, pp. 157–58.   2. Tr. Evelyn-White, p. 117.
3. Line numbering as in the OCT edn.

theus is even said to be Uranos,[4] the heavenly god and husband of Earth, while his mother in this connection is named Klymene, this Hesiodic name also becomes transparent. Regardless of whether it means "she who hears our prayers" or "the Illustrious One," it is the name of an underworld goddess who in Hesiod appears in the chorus of the daughters of Okeanos. Originally, Prometheus' father had a great wife: perhaps the Earth herself, but we also find mention of such names as Asia and Asope [5]—which may have been special names of a great goddess, as we shall see when we come to speak of Asia, the wife of Prometheus. Euphorion,[6] the learned Alexandrian poet, even knew of a very strange version of Prometheus' birth in which Hera was his mother. She was said to have borne him by a dark and impetuous son of the earth, the giant Eurymedon.[7]

The Brothers of Prometheus

T H E brothers whom Hesiod assigns to Prometheus circumscribe the dark and sorrowful realm of this family. He regards the story of Epimetheus as particularly edifying and tells it twice, in the *Theogony* (570–612) and in *Works and Days* (60–105). In the *Theogony* (512), he tells us that from the very first he "was a mischief to men who eat bread." [8] Epimetheus took as his wife the first woman, "the beautiful evil," whom Zeus had made for the ruin of men. He himself was condemned to become the first sufferer. But the situation is very strange.

---

4. Theon, scholium on Aratus 254, in Maass, p. 386, line 7.
5. Scholium on Apollonios Rhodios I 444 (ed. Wendel, p. 40) and Proklos, scholium on Hesiod's *Erga kai Hemerai* [*Works and Days*] 48 (in Gaisford, II, 76).
6. In J. U. Powell, *Collectanea Alexandrina*, p. 42.
7. Scholium on the Iliad XIV 295.   8. Tr. Evelyn-White, p. 117.

For it was through the folly of Epimetheus that mankind was to be punished: punished—and this too is strange—for the clever trick of Prometheus. And all this at a time when there were men but no "human race," because the first woman was, precisely, Pandora, the "beautiful evil." The catalogue poem bearing Hesiod's name relates that she was the mother of Deukalion, father of the human race.[9] According to this tradition, however, the father of Deukalion was not Epimetheus but Prometheus. How, we may ask with a trace of irony, can the wary Prometheus have let himself in for such folly? But our irony would be out of place if this is a vestige of an archaic myth. We might be more justified in asking whether Prometheus and Epimetheus may not originally have been a pair grown together, who engendered the human race with the first woman.[10]

The names Prometheus and Epimetheus are clearly related linguistically. The first means "he who knows in advance" and the second surely "he who learns afterward," both formed from the stem of the verb *mantháno* at a relatively early period, for the termination *-eus* is characteristic of old proper names, and later on the stem *méthē* (that we may postulate as an analagon to *léthē* beside *láthos*) had ceased to exist beside *máthos*. These transparent names seem to be early interpretations rather than the original names of mythological beings: they suggest the widely distributed folk tale of the two unequal brothers, a purely human tale or one at least which has become human. Prometheus also had other less transparent names and these—we shall soon become acquainted with them—are no doubt older. Moreover, in relation to Zeus, the wily Prometheus, as his story in Hesiod shows, is defi-

9. Scholium on Ap. Rhod. III 1086 (ed. Wendel, p. 248), from which the scholium on the Odyssey X 2 differs.
10. A parallel may be found in Kerényi, "The Trickster in Relation to Greek Mythology," in Radin, *The Trickster*, p. 181.

nitely one who learns afterward. His way of thinking is characterized by the same epithet as that of the Titan Kronos, who, like him, is only seemingly clever and is defeated by Zeus. Both are *ankylomêtai*, devious (*ankýlos*) in their thinking, but they are both caught in their own noose (*ankýlē*): a mentality which may unquestionably be called "Titanic" after its first-named representative. It implies all manner of deviousness, from lying and scheming to the cleverest inventions, but even the inventions always presuppose some deficiency in the trickster's mode of life. This deficiency relates the Titans to man and his limitations, showing them to be rooted in human reality. Regardless of whether Epimetheus was originally a single hybrid being or formed a mythological pair of twins with Prometheus, he clearly exemplifies human limitations: his craftiness is a complement to his stupidity.

Menoitios, whom Hesiod names among the brothers of Prometheus, is characterized in the *Theogony* not only by the violence of the Titans and earthly giants. According to his name, "he whom *oîtos,* mortal doom, awaits," he may have been the "first mortal." The doom that overtakes him as the son of Iapetos is that of his father. In the *Theogony* (514–16) we read: ". . . far-seeing Zeus struck him with a lurid thunderbolt and sent him down to Erebos because of his mad presumption and exceeding pride." [11]

Still more characteristic is the punishment of Atlas, the first-named brother, which is also described (517–20): "And Atlas through hard constraint upholds the wide heaven with unwearying head and arms, standing at the borders of the earth before the clear-voiced Hesperides; for this lot wise Zeus assigned to him." [12]

11. Tr. Evelyn-White, p. 117. On line 516:

εἶνεκ' ἀτασθαλίης τε καὶ ἠνορέης ὑπερόπλου

cf. pp. 27 f. 12. Tr. Evelyn-White, p. 117.

A cruel fate and an arduous charge, whose purpose it is to hold heaven and earth apart so that day and night may alternate and "time" can begin. Atlas is not by accident a brother of Prometheus. His cast of mind is indicated in the Odyssey (I 52); he is *oloóphron*, "baleful," an epithet which sums up all the crafty and dangerous characteristics which Hesiod attributes to Prometheus. His situation—charge and punishment in one—at the western edge of the Greek world corresponds exactly to that of the punished Prometheus at the eastern edge. Images of hardship and suffering, these two supply a frame to the sphere of temporal human existence. Hesiod is so struck by the obvious parallelism that he leaps abruptly from the narrative of the Prometheus mythologem to an account of the punishment, relating how Prometheus was cruelly chained to a pillar by Zeus himself (521–22): "And ready-witted Prometheus he bound with inextricable bonds, cruel chains, and drove a shaft through his middle" [13]—a scene conceivable in the *Titanomachia*, but unthinkable in Homer—and then the perpetual wound of Prometheus, which the eagle sent by the king of the gods perpetually renews (524–25): this bird "used to eat his [i.e., the Titan's] immortal liver; but by night the liver grew as much again everyway as the long-winged bird devoured in the whole day." [14]

There are archaic vase paintings which perhaps show this cruel form of chaining [V] or Prometheus only bound to the pillar, and across from him Atlas, the serpents of the Hesperides behind him indicating that he is in the Garden of the Hesperides [VI].

13. Ibid. 14. Ibid.

Prometheus' Wound

T O ask after the extrahuman prototype and model of this wounding of a god proves to be just as reasonable as in the case of Hera. Prometheus' wound is just as meaningful to us as the wound in Hera's breast, renewed each month as the moonlight vanishes from our eyes. Hera's wound was inflicted by darkness. With Prometheus it is the opposite. To those ancient peoples, including the Greeks, who practiced the form of soothsaying known as hepatoscopy, the liver, which in the Prometheus mythologem grows again at night, is the seat of the picture of the world that could be read from the night sky.[15] It is dark in color. According to Aischylos (*Prom.* 1025),[16] the eagle eats of its darkness— and it was also nocturnal in so far as it was regarded as the seat of the passions. The eagle of Zeus—little more than a metaphor for the sun, which Aischylos once invokes as the "bird of Zeus"[17]—appears with the day, to devour the liver. This suffering—day itself interpreted as the suffering of darkness—seems to assign Prometheus to the realm of darkness.

In the history of the Greeks, the liberation of Prometheus from his wound and indeed from his vulnerability—this development of a nocturnal god away from his nocturnal nature—seems to signify the transformation of an archaic view of the world which attached even more importance to the celestial occurrence itself, the decrease of dark-

---

15. C. O. Thulin, *Die Götter des Martianus Capella und der Bronzeleber von Piacenza*, pp. 16 f., and *Die etruskische Disciplin*, II, 20 ff., where Babylonian parallels are adduced as well as testimonies to the Greek practice of hepatoscopy, which in the scholium on Aisch. *Prom.* 484 (Stanley, p. 729) is traced back to Prometheus. See, in general, my *Griechische Miniaturen*, p. 190, n. 10, and *Asklepios*, p. xxv.

16. See n. 3, above.   17. *The Suppliant Maidens* 212 (tr. Smyth, p. 21).

ness, than to the suffering perpetuated by the mythological expression of this event in heaven, a transformation in which human existence, the soft counterpole to the hard sky, gained in importance. In human existence, "suffering" and "darkness" are so closely related that all processes in which the darkness plays a part—whether actively or passively —seem to involve suffering. Hesiod tells us of the liberation of Prometheus, the slaying of the eagle [IV, V]; however, he is not concerned with the sufferer, but with the undiminished rule of Zeus, the paternal order based on the maternal will (*Theogony* 526–34):

"That bird Herakles, the valiant son of shapely-ankled Alkmene, slew; and delivered the son of Iapetos from the cruel plague, and released him from his affliction—not without the will of Olympian Zeus who reigns on high, that the glory of Herakles the Theban-born might be yet greater than it was before over the plenteous earth. This, then, he regarded, and honoured his famous son; though he was angry, he ceased from the wrath which he had before because Prometheus matched himself in wit with the almighty son of Kronos." [18]

The Deeds of Prometheus

T H U S at the very beginning we learn the end of the story, the reconciliation of Zeus with Prometheus. Only then does Hesiod describe the acts of Prometheus which led to the final separation between the divine and the human spheres and the establishment of the human mode of existence. There were two original deeds: the invention of the sacrifice and the theft of fire. Here Hesiod had to relate primordial themes, to fit events belonging to the most remote mythology into the structure

18. Tr. Evelyn-White, pp. 117, 119.

of his Zeus world. We read on, taking every word of the Greek text very literally (535–70):

"For when the gods and mortal men disputed at Mekone, even then Prometheus was forward to cut up a great ox and set portions before them, trying to befool the mind of Zeus. Before the rest he set flesh and inner parts thick with fat upon the hide, covering them with an ox paunch; but for Zeus he put the white bones dressed up with cunning art and covered with shining fat. Then the father of men and of gods said to him:

"'Son of Iapetos, most glorious of all lords, good sir, how unfairly you have divided the portions!'

"So said Zeus, full of eternal counsel, rebuking him. But wily Prometheus answered him, smiling softly and not forgetting his cunning trick:

"'Zeus, most glorious and greatest of the eternal gods, take which ever of these portions your heart within you bids.' So he said, thinking trickery. But Zeus, full of eternal counsel, saw and failed not to perceive the trick, and in his heart he thought mischief against mortal men which also was to be fulfilled. With both hands he took up the white fat and was angry at heart, and wrath came to his spirit when he saw the white ox-bones craftily tricked out: and because of this the tribes of men upon earth burn white bones to the deathless gods upon fragrant altars. But Zeus who drives the clouds was greatly vexed and said to him:

"'Son of Iapetos, clever above all! So, sir, you have not yet forgotten your cunning arts!'

"So spake Zeus, full of eternal counsel, in anger; and from that time he was always mindful of the trick, and would not give the power of unwearying fire to the wretched race of mortal men who live on the earth. But the noble son of Iapetos outwitted him and stole the far-seen gleam of unwearying fire in a hollow fennel-stalk. And Zeus who thunders on high was stung in spirit, and his dear heart was angered when he saw amongst men the far-seen ray of fire. Forthwith he made an evil thing for men as the price of fire. . . ." [19]

The Original Sacrifice

T H I S story is based on the assumption that gods and men had not yet been separated by the "sundered power," as Pindar calls it (see p. 22). This *kekriména dýnamis* came about when in Mekone gods and men disputed (*ekrínonto*) in the sense of "separating" and "differentiating." Here we definitely have a pre-mythological de-cision contrasting with the Greek mythological view of the world, which was determined by the resulting polarity. And this situates Mekone, where the decision was made, in a special sphere. Geographically, this Place of Poppies (from *mékōn*, "poppy") was thought to be situated in the vicinity of the Peloponnesian city of Sikyon near Corinth, and mythologically in the realm of the poppy goddesses, Demeter and Persephone. Both notions may be correct; then Mekone would be a Sikyonian cult site of Demeter and Persephone, where Hesiod was told that the famous decision had taken place. It seems strange that the scene of an event which first ushered in our world should have been located in this very same world, but this is a paradox that occurs in all cosmogonic mythologems. For men always build their myths from elements of the concrete world they know, even when the myth is concerned with the genesis of the world—its creation or establishment.

19. Ibid., pp. 119, 121, modified.

The invention and first offering of the characteristic sacrifice of a religion may well be regarded as an act of world creation or at least as an act establishing the prevailing world order. If we were interested in parallels—and to find parallels is child's play compared to the task of bringing out the full meaning of the texts—we might easily find clear examples in the history of religions, particularly those of India. Even the Christian sacrifice of the Mass must be interpreted as the act by which the Christian world order was established. Once Christ's action at the Last Supper took on the significance of a prototypical ritual act, it became a foundation sacrifice, the great sacrifice by which the world of salvation was established. However, this example interests us here chiefly for the contrast it presents with the sacrifice of Prometheus: the foundation sacrifice of the Christian world was intended to signify a reconciliation, the resolution of a tension, an annulment as it were of the difference between God and man. It is quite the contrary with the act of Prometheus by which the narrator sought to explain why, in certain sacrifices of the Greeks, the gods received the more attractive but less palatable portions.[20]

Hesiod had only to hint at the prototypical character of this act of Prometheus, for it was perfectly obvious in a world where at every sacrifice the gods received chiefly fat and bones, while the sacrificers took most of the meat and entrails. A strange division! Yet every division presupposes a whole to be divided and a common bond between those who do the dividing. And this brings us to still another prerequisite for division: a distinction between the sharers. The idea of the Greek sacrifice takes in both: the distinction and the common bond between gods and men. Hesiod puts this idea of the sacrifice, with its implica-

---

20. This point of view is argued in opposition to the so-called "positivistic" interpretation in Kerényi, *Niobe,* pp. 40 ff., where ethnological parallels are also adduced.

tion of balance and freedom from conflict, in the age of gold.[21] Hesiod characterizes the sacrifice as an act of establishment, as the foundation of our world, by stressing the difference in the division and explaining it on the basis of a contest. After the division, the world came into being—a world in which gods and men were absolutely different. And in Hesiod's eyes this was perfectly just, because men are exactly as they showed themselves to be in their sacrificing: deceived deceivers. Even if Hesiod had based his mythological view of the world not on a tradition but on a doctrine to be derived from the Greek sacrifice, it would be grounded in an inherently justifiable conception of man's nature.

Pre-Hesiodic Elements in Hesiod

B U T Hesiod's narrative contains strange features which show us from the start how dependent he was on mythological traditions that he was obliged to integrate with his Zeus world. Strange enough was the first presupposition of his separation narrative, an original undivided state, the absence of any absolute difference between gods and men. Another, of which we shall have more to say later on, is the tacit identification of the cause of Prometheus with that of men. "For when the gods and mortal men disputed at Mekone," the tale begins, Prometheus (not men!) apportioned the ox. Prometheus took up the contest with the gods. But it was men who had to suffer the consequence of his defeat. When he makes common cause with men and steals the fire for them (Hesiod regards this intervention as so self-evident that he does not say so much as a word to account for it), Epimetheus (as we have al-

21. Hesiod in Rzach, fr. 82. Cf. Pausanias VIII 2 4; Catullus 64 384–86. Kerényi, *The Religion of the Greeks and Romans*, p. 190; on the sacrifice of Prometheus in connection with the idea of the Greek sacrifice, ibid., pp. 189 ff.

ready related) receives the first woman as punishment. But seen in a certain light, the two strange features—the undifferentiated character of the group Prometheus–Epimetheus–human-race and the original undifferentiatedness of gods and men—annul one another. This they do if we suppose that there was once a mythologem in which the two brothers, or the one primordial Prometheus-Epimetheus as divine advocate, precursor or ancestor of the human race, alone confronted the celestial gods: in this case, the contest was solely *among gods*, still undifferentiated in their divinity, and this seems precisely to have been the pre-Hesiodic situation.

The presence of "mortal men" in Hesiod's narrative of contest and division is required not by the content but by the form. The very way in which it is expressed is purely conventional: where men are mentioned in the epic language, it is already as "those who inhabit the earth far and wide." [22] Essentially, they are mentioned in the same way as the later cult site of Mekone, as belonging to the world. The world is still in process of creation, but it would be impossible to speak of it intelligibly were one to be consistent and think away its present inhabitants. The polarity "gods and men" was simply an inherent part of the Greek vision of the world. Not even the archaic philosopher who proclaimed the existence of a single God, whose existence excludes all other gods and admits of no comparison whatever with mortal men: not even Xenophanes could express himself without this polarity. The epic language and the view of the world inherent in it compelled him to speak inconsistently. "There is one god," his famous saying runs, "among gods and men the greatest." [23] Our translation speaks of men as the

22. οἳ ἐπὶ χθονὶ ναιετάουσιν.
23. Diels, fr. 23 (an English version in Freeman, p. 23).
    εἷς θεὸς ἔν τε θεοῖσι καὶ ἀνθρώποισι μέγιστος.

"wretched" on the basis of a reading introduced in modern times: *meléoisi*. The manuscripts have instead *meliēisi*, "ashes," or perhaps more correctly *melíoisi*, "ash men." According to *Works and Days* (145), Zeus created the men of the brazen age from the wood of the ash: this was not an actual creation of men but the shaping of a generation of mankind and thereby of an era. In the *Theogony* (187), Hesiod relates only how the *Meliai*, the ash nymphs, sprang from the blood of Uranos—they had no need of fire;[24] as for men, they are somehow already there when Prometheus, as though it were the most natural thing in the world, champions their cause. What leads him to do so we are not told.

The scene we have described presupposes the polarity of the Greek world view, here mankind, there the gods. It is accepted and stated, but plays no further role. Prometheus and Zeus alone confront one another like two pristine mythological beings who come together and engage in a contest, not for any reason known to human psychology but because they are as they are and cannot be otherwise. The wily Prometheus, whose nature and existential weakness it is to "think deviously," gives the contest its direction, even if he does not provoke it. Replying with a gentle smile to the reproaches of Zeus,[25] he reminds us of Hermes more than of any other god. But Hermes' deception springs from a creative art, which enriches the divinity of the world with playful magic.[26] In the original deception of Prometheus, a basic flaw in the character of Prometheus is the source of grave shortcomings in man.

---

24. Those who suppose that Hesiod meant to say that Zeus gave the ashes—the trees, not the nymphs—no fire, lest men should make tinderboxes from ash wood, are imputing a very "devious thought" to the poet!

25. *Theogony* 547: ἧκ' ἐπιμειδήσας.   26. Kerényi, *Hermes der Seelenführer*.

The Mind of Zeus

I N Hesiod the strange behavior of Zeus throws a bright light on the shortcomings of Prometheus. Not only is Zeus, for Hesiod, "full of eternal counsel" [27]—repeatedly and emphatically so called—but, moreover, the whole scene, from the very start, is so constructed as to emphasize the "mind," the *noûs* of Zeus. The epithet attached to this perfectly mirroring *noûs* in the Iliad (XV 461) is *pýkinos*, "close-knit"; nothing can escape it.[28] By undertaking to "deceive Zeus' mind," Prometheus shows himself to be one who necessarily remains wanting, who can never be rewarded by complete success. "Zeus, full of eternal counsel, saw through the stratagem and noted it well." [29] Seeing through the deception, he lets himself be cheated—once again in a manner consonant with the *Titanomachia* but not with Homer, in the old "Titanic style"—but not deceived. In respect to his *noûs*, which is over all things, that would be impossible, for his "mind" is precisely like a mirror that takes in everything without distortion and reflects it. It contains a motionless image of all being, of all deeds good and bad with their consequences, hence it is free from all will or desire to change anything. Prometheus himself is thus mirrored; the mind of Zeus sees the futility of his desire to change things, of the action of one not endowed with the "mind" of Zeus, a being whose deficient nature manifestly prevents him from accepting being as it is.

27. ἄφθιτα μήδεα εἰδώς.
28. Philippson, *Untersuchungen über den griechischen Mythos,* p. 27, n. 7. On the following cf. Kerényi, *Die antike Religion,* 3rd edn., p. 114, and pp. 192 f. of the English edition, *The Religion of the Greeks and Romans.*
29. *Theogony* 550–51.

Parallel in 'Works and Days'

T H E transition does not seem too abrupt when suddenly Hesiod turns to the effect upon mankind of Prometheus' crime. Men, too, would like, by guile and invention, to modify the being over which their mind does not stand like a mirror but which they must bear. How their life would be if this were not so, Hesiod tells us in *Works and Days* (42–59), where he likewise celebrates the victory of Zeus.

"For the gods keep hidden from men the means of life. Else you would easily do work enough in a day to supply you for a full year even without working; soon would you put away your rudder over the smoke, and the fields worked by ox and sturdy mule would run to waste. But Zeus in the anger of his heart hid it, because Prometheus the crafty deceived him; therefore he planned sorrow and mischief against men. He hid fire; but that the noble son of Iapetos stole again for men from Zeus the counsellor in a hollow fennel-stalk, so that Zeus who delights in thunder did not see it. But afterwards Zeus who gathers the clouds said to him in anger:

" 'Son of Iapetos, surpassing all in cunning, you are glad that you have outwitted me and stolen fire—a great plague to you yourself and to men that shall be. But I will give men as the price for fire an evil thing in which they may all be glad of heart while they embrace their own destruction.' " [30]

The victory of Zeus becomes complete only with the creation of the "evil thing in which they may all be glad of heart"—namely, woman.

30. Tr. Evelyn-White, pp. 5, 7.

Hesiod repeatedly stresses his belief that the stern order of the Zeus world is based equally on the Epimethean, masculine desire for woman and upon a trait of man that we have seen to be at once Promethean and universally human: the impulse to modify the world by crafty inventiveness. But still the picture is not clear to us, because the exact nature of the relation between Prometheus and mankind, which for Hesiod was defined by a mythological tradition, eludes the modern reader. The daily suffering of the nocturnal Prometheus and his benevolent theft of fire are aspects of an all-too-human being who, according to Greek conceptions, was Titanic. And now, after our reading of Hesiod, we may return to the question upon which we touched in the discussion of Goethe that served as a preamble to the present study: What is this being who is so close to mankind? Is he a god, a Titan, or a man? Aischylos expressly calls him a god, and for all three of the great Greek tragic poets he was a Titan.[31] For a more precise picture of the Greek view of Prometheus we must consult the prose tradition.

31. Apart from Aischylos: Sophokles, *Oedipus at Colonus* 56 (cf. LCL edn., p. 150); Euripides, *Ion* 455 (cf. LCL edn., IV, 46), *The Phoenician Maidens* 1122 (ibid., III, 438).

IV. ARCHAIC PROMETHEUS MYTHOLOGY

'The Herald of the Titans'

WHAT TRAIT of Prometheus could be contrasted with the nature of Zeus? To what sort of being did it belong? The trait in question was a source of corruption to mankind but also of salvation, providing man with fire and the means of perpetuating his existence. But what sort of being was the corrupter and savior? We find a sort of answer in Hesychios,[1] the Greek lexicographer and collector of "glosses," unusual expressions, and names employed in ancient texts. According to him, the word "Ithas" meant "the Herald of the Titans, Prometheus, whom others call Ithax." In what text, we now ask, was Prometheus called Ithas and Ithax—perhaps merely different readings for the same name—and "herald of the Titans"? In view of all we know today about the *Titanomachia* (in part set forth above) it seems certain that the gloss stems from this very work or, if there were several works of like content, from one of them. But these names are not transparent; they cannot be interpreted with certainty. Ithas suggests *ithagenḗs*, a Greek word which Hesychios translates as "autochthonous," while Ithax recalls Ithakē, the island of Odysseus, and Ithakos, the name of an artist who lived there (Odyssey XVII 207). The idea of a kinship with Odysseus the Ithacan comes to mind, and indeed he is the most Promethean of all Homer's heroes. The ancient artists make the heads of Prometheus and Odysseus strikingly alike, both of them crafty, both of them resembling Hermes more than any other god, both wearing the pointed cap of an artist or artisan, rather an odd head covering for a Homeric

---

1. *Lexicon* (ed. Schmidt), s.v. Ἴθας.

hero.[2] Hephaistos and the Kabeiroi are also shown wearing this type of cap.

"Herald of the Titans" actually implies something more than a kinship between the Promethean cast of mind—which we have thus far called Titanic because of the relation between Prometheus and Kronos, the other "devious thinker"—and that of Hermes, whose grandson was Odysseus. Both elements play a part: he was a Titan and among all the Titans it was he who inevitably came to the mind of a poet whose narrative called for a messenger among the Titanic host. The herald of the gods was Hermes. His was the function and character of one traveling eternally back and forth, connecting antithetical realms, Olympos and Hades. He was a mediator who hovered in the mid-zone, between the heavens and the realm of the dead. Mortal heralds imitated the immortals, drawing confidence in their calling from the reality that Hermes represented for them. The Titanic world of the gods, as it is gradually becoming known to us through oriental parallels, is wild enough, but it suggests astral bodies more than human beings. Such names as Hyperion, "the Upper," corresponding to the Latin *superior,* Koios—related to *koia,* "sphere"—Krios, perhaps the celestial Ram, listed by Hesiod, who took them from the Greek tradition, suggest the starry heavens. Not only Hyperion, father of Helios, but also in all likelihood Kronos shows a resemblance to the sun. To be sure, Kronos carried out his bloody primordial act, the separation of the original parents, with a sickle, image of the new moon, but the act itself may well be regarded as solar. Saturn, the planet assigned to him, is also known in Greek as *Helíou astér,* "Star of the Sun."[3] Still less than that of Hermes can the

---

2. Kerényi, *Heroes*, p. 328.

3. Plato, *Epinomis* 987 c, as another reading for Κρόνου ἀστήρ. Franz Boll, in "Kronos-Helios," *Arch RW,* XIX (1916–19), pp. 342 ff., shows it to be based on an old tradition.

situation of Prometheus as messenger of the Titans be derived merely from human conditions; it must—and this throws light also on the function and character of Hermes—be traced back to conditions in heaven.

Prometheus, like the moonlike Hera, bears a wound that is perpetually renewed. It does not point to a waning in winter like that other wound, interwoven with human existence, which is also discernible in the heavens: the wounding of the sun. Our assumption that *human existence* was the chief determinant of these mythical figures, because it is no doubt the prevailing viewpoint of existing human beings at all times, distinguishes our mode of observing and interpreting ancient mythology from all previous attempts characterized by astral or "naturist" theories.[4] In the figure of Prometheus, being wounded coincides with the position of the mediator, with the hovering-in-the-middle typical of the messenger and—in the world as seen by men—of the moon. He is a moonlike being, but not wholly identical with the astronomical moon, and indeed no one figure exhausts the moon as a source of mythological possibilities. He was chosen as herald because he was the one moonlike being among the Titans. However, the moon is bright and dark, and Prometheus belongs to the darkness. The night heals him, while each day wounds him anew. In this he differs essentially from Hermes, the lunar messenger among the Olympians. Hermes, too, is nocturnal and, like the moon, a wanderer, but he belongs to the rising light of the sun and of life, and has nothing to do with the dark side of life. The more aware we become of the kinship between Prometheus and Hermes and the better we grasp the common element in their situa-

---

4. This mode has been thus misunderstood by L. Séchan, *Le Mythe de Prométhée,* p. 12, and others who have failed to take note of the philosophical transformation of scientific attitudes.

tion and their function in the divine world, the more keenly we perceive the radical difference between these two moonlike beings. The Olympian messenger has his place among the heavenly gods, while Prometheus, the "herald of the Titans," is clearly related to mankind.

Prometheus and Hermes

W H A T is common to Hermes and Prometheus remains in the realm of those primordial deeds which do not cut through and separate, like that of Kronos, but which cut or break into the world of living growth, which strike wounds in the divine environment. But these are wounds indispensable to human existence; from them surges life, something divine which unites the wounded ones with the gods who were disturbed and offended by the incursion. The act which reunited was the sacrifice. Its necessary presupposition was two sacrilegious acts of incursion into the living growth of the environment. The first sacrilege, which, however, was a blessing to those in search of nourishment, was the slaying of the beast, whose flesh was served up as a sacrifice for the benefit of gods and men. The other primordial act was the acquisition of fire, which is more familiar to us as sacred sacrificial fire than as a living and growing element in our environment. This sacred nature of fire, which it shares with all the living things that grow in man's environment and provide him with sustenance, explains why the acquisition of fire was experienced as theft, as desecration.

Both primordial acts, as well as the invention of the sacrifice which crowns and expiates them, are attributed both to Prometheus and to Hermes. They are related also of Phoroneus, the primordial man who founded the human community at Argos.[5] The tradition relates expressly that Prometheus was the first to have killed an ox, the sacrificial beast.[6] Hesiod does not mention this explicitly. In Hesiod, the theft of fire is detached from its context: slaying the animal—stealing fire—first sacrifice. He represents it as a new beneficent sacrilege,[7] although the original sacrilegious-sacred act embraced all three: the fire is stolen from the gods as a means of offering up a sacrifice.[8] But in Hesiod another logical context remains unbroken: a sacrifice presupposes sacrificers as well as receivers, and Hesiod proceeds on the assumption that men are already in existence, participating in the sacrifice. The above-mentioned context is still in force in the Homeric hymn to Hermes (IV 1–137): Hermes, the newborn and already dangerous god, steals the oxen of Apollo, invents a means of kindling fire with a tinderbox of laurel wood, kills two oxen, and establishes the sacrifice to the twelve gods, including himself.[9] But here, as in related mythologems of other peoples, no mention is made of men as sacrificers. Often the sacrificers and the beneficiaries of the sacrifice are identical. In the Homeric hymn to Hermes, the identity is not even mystical, for the sacrifice is invented before the existence of men. Hermes did not represent mankind, but Prometheus did.

Prometheus is distinguished from the other Titans by his close kinship with Hermes. He is distinguished from Hermes in turn by his bond with mankind and by traits in keeping with the human mode of existence: by his punishment and its cause, the sacrilege attaching to his act as the first sacrificer. And so Prometheus stands before us: a moon-

5. Kerényi, *Gods*, p. 222.
6. Pliny, *Natural History* VII 209: *Prometheus bovem primus occidit.*
7. *Works and Days* 51–52, *Theogony* 565–66.
8. S. Eitrem, "De Prometheo," *Eranos* (Göteborg), XLIV (1946), 14 ff.
9. Kerényi, *Gods*, p. 164.

like being, but not a luminous one, embodying the darkness of the dark moon, and also bearing marks of human existence; one compelled by his own shortcomings to offend against his environment and his companions in growth; who in so doing employs devious, crooked thinking (for in the world of growth the pathways are naturally crooked); inevitably, a wounder and a wounded one. These are among his human characteristics. The cosmic situation of a dark moonlike being of this kind is that of the new moon, whence rises the sickle—in mythical tales also taking the form of an ax (we shall see it in the hand of Prometheus). The women who are associated with Prometheus in various traditions delimit his situation in the heavens.

Women of Prometheus

I N this study we shall not speak of Pandora, who requires special treatment.[10] Klymene, a wife of Prometheus (named as his mother in Hesiod), points to the great goddess of the underworld. Pronoë—if a wife of Prometheus was really so called [11]—would be the feminine form of Prometheus, meaning "she who knows in advance, who provides." The masculine form Pronoös occurrs in the genealogy of Hellen, ancestor of the Greeks, who was descended from Prometheus.[12] It is clearly a synonymous name for Prometheus. However, these are not real names but rather explanatory epithets for the Titan Ithas or Ithax.

---

10. See the narratives in Kerényi, *Gods,* pp. 216–20.

11. The scholium on the Odyssey X 2 has Klymene and Pryleie, perhaps instead of Pronoë.

12. Hekataios in Jacoby, *Die Fragmente der griechischen Historiker,* 1 F 13 (I, 10).

The "place" of Prometheus is defined by a more expressive group of names: by Kelaino [13] on the one side and on the other by Pyrrha (daughter of Epimetheus), Asia, Hesione. Kelaino means "the Dark One," Pyrrha "the Golden-Blond One," and Asia would assuredly not have become the name for the Orient if it had not originally signified "the Eastern" or the "Morninglike" or been related in some other way to what, from the Greek point of view, was the land of the rising sun. Like a number of the earlier great goddesses in Hesiod,[14] Asia was included among the daughters of Okeanos, while Hyginus numbers her among the Nereids, the daughters of the other ancient sea-god. Herodotus [15] has it that the wife of Prometheus bore this name and at the same time tells us that the eastern continent had taken its name from none other than her. As Athena Asia, this goddess was revered in Laconia.[16] With Athene, as we shall soon see, Prometheus had close ties. And the name seems to have been borne by a divine lady whose cult, along with that of the *Theia mater*, is attested in a Mycenaean document from Pylos.[17] It is not likely that Hesione—the spouse named in *Prometheus Bound* (560)—was taken to mean the same as Asia. However, she was connected with Troy; Hesione was the daughter of the first king, who built that famous oriental city with the help of divine servitors.[18] All these goddesses evoke dawn or darkness. Darkness and dawn define the situation of the new moon when it leaves the darkness and yet in a sense carries darkness along with it as its own invisible complement. This is the "place," the celestial background, of Prometheus. But it should not be supposed that any phenomenon in the heavens can exhaust his meaning. The name of another wife of

13. Tzetzes in his commentary on Lykophron 132 (I, 399).
14. *Theogony* 359; Hyginus, *Fabulae*, Preface (Genealogiae).   15. IV 45 3.
16. Pausanias III 24 7.   17. Fr 1206: po-ti-ni-ya a-si-vi-ya.
18. Kerényi, *Heroes*, p. 160.

Prometheus, whom we have not yet mentioned, Axiothea,[19] connects him with beings who are anything but celestial. The first part of the name—an archaic ritual invocation, *axios,* "worthy"—is characteristically contained in such Kabeirian names as Axieros, Axiokersos, Axiokersa.[20]

Prometheus among the Kabeiroi

T H E figure of Prometheus is not the only example of contact between the Titans and the Kabeiroi. This is attested in the inscription of Imbros,[21] which, in an invocation of the Kabeiroi, lists the Hesiodic series of the great Titans, the sons of Uranos, with the exception of Okeanos: Koios, Krios, Hyperion, Iapetos, Kronos.[22] In the sixth century B.C. the Orphic theologian and poet Onomakritos had already undertaken, surely not without reason and evidently not without success, to identify the Titans with the Kabeiroi. He attributed the murder and dismemberment of the child Dionysos to the Titans.[23] If it is asked what led him to do so, we need only recall that two brothers from among the Kabeiroi had committed a similar murder on the person of their younger brother.[24] The name of the Titans and of the Kabeiroi as well is tainted with primordial crime. Of course mysteries—rites of purification and initiation—are also associated with the Kabeiroi.[25] According to the legend of the founding of the Kabeirion near Thebes, there had once been a city on this site, inhabited by men named Kabeiraioi after the place.[26] To one of these original inhabitants, Prometheus, and to his son

19. Tzetzes, 283 (II, 988).   20. Kerényi, *Gods,* p. 87.
21. *Inscriptiones Graecae* XII 8 74 (p. 33).   22. Kerényi, *Gods,* p. 21.
23. Pausanias VIII 37 5. Cf Kerényi, *Der frühe Dionysos,* p. 36.
24. Kerényi, *Gods,* p. 86.
25. Kerényi, "The Mysteries of the Kabeiroi," pp. 42 ff.
26. Pausanias IX 25 6.

Aitnaios, Demeter brought the mysteries. This constitutes the beginning of a fairly long pseudohistorical *narratif à clé*, of a type that was permitted in connection with the mysteries: most of the participants are referred to by pseudonyms which were transparent to the initiates, and are even quite clear to us. Aitnaios, the "Aetnan," can only be Hephaistos (after his Sicilian mountain). Here he is mentioned as a Kabeiros, and no doubt he passed as such on his own island of Lemnos, in the ancient cultic sphere of the Kabeiroi. He was the ancestor of certain Kabeiroi who were said to have been called Hephaistoi after him:[27] these were assuredly those Kabeiroi who, like Hephaistos, practiced the art of the blacksmith and carried hammers.

Thus Prometheus, who among the Titans was only the son of Iapetos, a mere herald and rather a second-rank figure, proves to have been the most venerable of the Kabeiroi, their father and ancestor. It can scarcely be an accident that his cult in Athens reflects the same relation to Hephaistos. Here the two gods were worshiped along with Pallas Athene in the age-old sacred precinct of the Academy. An ancient relief at the entrance to the sanctuary represented Prometheus as the older, Hephaistos as the younger god. This should not necessarily be taken to mean that the cult of Prometheus was the older one. A hierarchical relation between a powerful father and a son who reveres and even serves him is not only related by the genealogists but is also represented in the cult and is typical for the Kabeiroi. Just as in Athens Hephaistos was the son of Prometheus, so the boy Kadmilos occupied this position on Lemnos.[28] But it is only Hephaistos who occurs in Homer. The great epic poet, who passes over so many archaic elements

27. Gloss of the learned patriarch Photios (*Lexikon*, ed. Naber, I, 302), who also calls them Τιτᾶνες.
28. I.e., Kadmilos was the son of Hephaistos. Kerényi, *Gods*, p. 87.

of the Greek religion, makes no mention of Prometheus. Thus, although in a number of extremely archaic contexts Hephaistos takes the place of Prometheus, it is still quite possible that he is only the successor of this particular mysterious Titan. An Attic vase painting of the fifth century shows Prometheus standing before Hera [VII] as though to confirm our theory, based on their mythological characteristics, of an association between these two beings. This fits in with the more infrequent and perhaps more secret tradition unearthed by the poet Euphorion,[29] one of the learned Alexandrians, to the effect that Hera was the mother of Prometheus, having been raped by the giant Eurymedon, a son of the Earth, whose name signifies "he who rules far and wide." But the tradition that became classical makes Hephaistos the son who is particularly close to Hera.

A similar situation is disclosed in the relation of the two to Pallas Athene. Both Prometheus and Hephaistos were said to have pursued her with their love.[30] And another, likewise archaic tale, the story of Athene's birth, helps us to guess which of them was originally associated with the daughter of Zeus. Which of the two split the head of Zeus in order that Pallas should be born from it: Prometheus or Hephaistos? The story is told of them both.[31] The primordial and original instrument employed was the ax. And certain versions even put it into the hand of Hephaistos, though in other traditions he performs his act of midwifery with a hammer. In the hand of Prometheus, the sacrificer, the ax is meaningful; and it has meaning also in the new-moon situation with which the great festivals of the goddess in Athens were connected.[32] This primordial deed, this cutting and breaking into what

29. In Powell, *Collect. Alex.,* p. 42.
30. Jacoby, *FGrHist,* 76 F 47 (II, sec. a, 150); Kerényi, *Gods,* p. 123.
31. Kerényi, *Gods,* p. 120.   32. Kerényi, *Die Jungfrau und Mutter,* p. 41.

was most sacred, was also a necessary crime: a sacred sacrilege, of which Homeric poetry says nothing but which Hesiod relates, though without mentioning the impetuous "deliverer." [33] Earlier in the present chapter (p. 57) we referred to a more gruesome sacred act performed by Prometheus among the Kabeiroi. Two brothers were said to have cut off the head of a third brother and wrapped it in a purple cloth: a mystery whose significance was kept secret but was assuredly highly religious.

Titans and Kabeiroi

B U T what can it mean that the same mythological beings should now be called "Titans" and now "Kabeiroi"? Though Onomakritos put the Titans in the place of the Kabeiroi, he did not regard the two as identical. The Imbros inscription, which cites all the great Titans in the series of the Kabeiroi, and the lexicon of Photios,[34] which states without distinction that the Kabeiroi are "Hephaistoi" or "Titans," bear witness to the progressive assimilation of these concepts and the original difference between them. To what extent this assimilation can have been based on living mythology we learn from the figure of Prometheus, who for particular reasons, inherent in his nature, is assigned both to the Titans and to the Kabeiroi. In the world view of Greek mythology, the Titans—aside from Okeanos, who for Homer was still the "Origin of all Beings" (Iliad XIV 246) and only for Hesiod became one Titan among others—belonged to the heavenly pole. They are the older in-

33. *Theogony* 924.
34. See n. 27 above.

habitants of heaven, who were there before the Olympian gods. This should not be taken to mean that in Greece itself they were worshiped before the Olympians, but only that in the Greek cosmogonies known to us they were represented as having been heavenly gods before the rule of Zeus was established in heaven and on earth. They are the primordial beings who were gods before the gods, at home in heaven like constellations, most of them in fact violently solar but including in their midst the moonlike Prometheus.

As for the Kabeiroi, we may say this much with certainty: that they also were primordial beings, belonging more to the other pole. According to the above-mentioned narrative from the Kabeirion in Thebes, they were the original men. In a famous vase painting from the sanctuary [Xb], the original male representatives of the human race, Protolaos and Mitos—"the First Man" and "Seed"—are represented as wild primordial men facing the great Dionysian Kabeiros and the Boy (Pais) who serves him. How could the story of a primordial city of the Kabeiroi and its inhabitants have arisen if the Kabeiroi had not been regarded as primordial beings who were men before men? And yet Pausanias, in recounting the legend, says that he is not permitted to reveal who the Kabeiroi actually were. This can only be taken to support the usual tradition according to which the Kabeiroi scarcely differed from the Titans in divinity. As gods, they belonged to the dark sphere whence life arose; their extreme masculinity made them—examined more closely, their function as primordial men must be interpreted in this light—the precursors of the earthly generations of men.

And thus Prometheus, the dark moonlike being among the Titans, with the all-too-masculine and simple-minded brother Epimetheus—both of them male and yet representatives of the human race over against the luminous gods of heaven—finds his exact place as one of the Kabeiroi in Greek mythology. A god like Hermes (equivalent of the Pais or Kadmilos) and Hephaistos, who were both Kabeiroi, the son of Iapetos fills the place, at the human counterpole of the divine world, which in non-Greek mythology is occupied by a divine primordial man.

V. METHODOLOGICAL INTERMEZZO

The Limits of Reconstruction

B Y   F O L L O W I N G in the traces of the ancient mythologizing mind, a modern can form a living picture of a mythological figure, even so strange a one as Ithax, herald of the Titans, one of the Kabeiroi—also named Prometheus after his most prominent trait—and, finally, the dark moon filled like a cup with humanity. For the ancient cosmos, determined by two poles—man and his environment, interwoven to form a "world"—*still exists*. It is the *world of men*, taking the form of mythological figures compounded of vision, dream, and poetry.

The traditions concerning such figures have two principal components—the content, the myth itself, and inseparably bound up with the content, the manner of its presentation. It may be presented in any number of ways. The essential is that we possess at least one of these presentations. The myth is the content, but it stands before us as a work. The presentation is always a work.[1] What once stood there as a work in its Greek particularity—and stood there not only once but several times in many works—can be reconstructed only from the standpoint of its content: in so far as the content is a fragment of the world that addresses us in human terms. The more the conscious creation of the artist predominates over this fragment of the world, the less the work can be constructed from hints and a few literary fragments.

---

1. Kerényi, "Werk und Mythos," in *Griechische Miniaturen,* p. 139.

How Much Can Be Known

W E must now approach the Prometheus plays of Aischylos, of which only the *Prometheus Bound* has been preserved in its entirety. The scientific literature on the subject begins with Friedrich Gottlieb Welcker. More than a century ago, in 1824, this celebrated mythologist and philologist wrote an impressive tome entitled: *Die Aeschylische Trilogie Prometheus und die Kabirienweihe zu Lemnos, nebst Winken über die Trilogie des Aeschylus überhaupt.*[2] In this work he attempted to reconstruct the content of all the trilogies of Aischylos. Two years later he published another, scarcely smaller volume entitled: *Nachtrag zu der Schrift über die Aeschylische Trilogie nebst einer Abhandlung über das Satyrspiel.*[3] The second work was intended chiefly as a refutation of the criticism raised against the first. Welcker inaugurated a school. Since then there have been repeated attempts at philological reconstruction, which, like Welcker's, have provoked a good deal of criticism, for they often exceed the limits of the knowable. There is no need to dwell on this school, which has long ceased to concern itself with what is important or even of interest to human beings and shows a distinct preference for speculations that are quite indemonstrable. There is scarcely any need to refute "laws of form" devised with a view to making the impossible possible and to recovering what has been lost forever. Even to draw inferences from the "structure of the trilogy," which can be observed only in the *Oresteia,* the one trilogy that has

2. "The Prometheus Trilogy of Aeschylus and the Kabirian Mysteries on Lemnos, Accompanied by Certain Remarks on the Trilogies of Aeschylus in General."
3. "Supplement to the Book on the Trilogies of Aeschylus, Including a Treatise on the Satyric Drama."

come down to us in its entirety, is pure mental gymnastics. And totally groundless are all inferences in regard to the history of dramatic poetry since Thespis that have been drawn from the incomplete lists of plays and from grammarians' notations that have accidentally been preserved.

All that can be known about what was actually enacted on the stage is what we read in the extant dramatic texts, in quotations from the plays, and on scraps of papyri. In Goethe's time ancient papyrus books were unheard of. The most that could be done in the way of reconstruction was to apply disciplined thinking to the traditional material, and in that direction Welcker went as far as possible. Today we have been awakened to a richer and more concrete knowledge of antiquity by a "material" tradition that was previously not conceivable. There is much new material to read, not only the papyrus fragments but also the archaeological finds, above all the vase paintings, which give us an immediate record that is only beginning to open to us. We are becoming better acquainted not only with the forms but with the content as well. The formal indications that scholars look for in texts in order to arrive at subtle conclusions about things that are beyond our knowledge result only too frequently from accidents of transmission. Consequently they provide exceedingly uncertain foundations for knowledge. Indications of this sort would have value only if the material from which they were drawn were complete, for example, the author's whole work and numerous other examples from the literature of his time. And when is that possible? On the basis of fortuitous indications of this kind, attempts have been made to disprove Aischylos' authorship of the *Prometheus Bound,* a work which in the whole tradition has never been attributed to anyone else. Such scholarship is subject to the utmost caution, and equally questionable are attempts to assign to

Aischylos fragments dealing with the world after the acquisition of fire.

It seems to me that such caution has actually been shown by the editor of one fragment, Oxyrhynchus Papyrus 2245.[4] In this case, Aischylos surely seems to be the most likely author, for we know that he wrote at least four plays on Prometheus: apart from the *Prometheus Bound* (*Prometheus Desmotes*), there was a *Prometheus Delivered* (*Prometheus Lyomenos*), a *Prometheus the Fire Bringer* (*Prometheus Pyrphoros*), and a *Prometheus the Fire Kindler* (*Prometheus Pyrkaeus*). The last was assuredly a satyric drama, performed in 472 B.C. along with the tragedies *Phineus, The Persians*, and *Glaukos of Potniai*. In that connection it was mentioned simply as "Prometheus" precisely because it was the first of the series and had no need to be distinguished from the poet's other Prometheus plays, which had not yet been written. We have vase paintings showing Prometheus—on one of them his name is inscribed—surrounded by satyrs and holding the narthex stalk containing the fire he had just stolen [VIII, IX, Xa]. These can only be dated between 440 and 420,[5] and Aischylos died in 456. We must conclude that thirty years after the appearance of his first Prometheus play its theme still retained its attraction for vase painters. Was the *Pyrkaeus* performed again at this time? Or had plays about the appearance of fire and its effects on the earth been written since Aischylos? The argument of the *Desmotes* tells us that apart from Aischylos only Sophokles had employed this theme. But we have no such information regarding the other Prometheus plays. Incalculable possibilities remain open, both for the Oxyrhynchus fragment and for the Heidelberg Papyrus 185. One critic has

4. Lobel, in *The Oxyrhynchus Papyri*, XX, fr. 1.
5. Beazley, "Prometheus Fire-Lighter," *AJA,* XLIII (1939), 618–39.

tried to identify the latter as a part of the *Lyomenos* [6] and another as stemming from the *Pyrphoros:* [7] we shall never *know,* unless perhaps some new material comes to light. It is, rather, the content that merits our attention.

What Is Communicable

T O D A Y it has become possible to achieve a richer and more concrete view of the Greek world than was conceivable in earlier generations. The mythological dimension of this view can wholly escape no one who does not persist in breaking down the total picture into specialized groups—one of these being "the religious." The new view of the Greek world has not yet been achieved by all those who are occupied with the various branches of specialization, nor is it the final and definitive view. Welcker's experience was similar to ours, for by considering literature, art, and mythology in one he arrived at a richer and more concrete picture than his predecessors. We have gone far beyond Welcker, but it is interesting to note that he clearly recognized and stated the most important element in the new situation of the science of antiquity. Here it seems worth our while to quote a passage from Welcker's "Supplement" on the trilogy of Aischylos, in which he speaks of the role of the mythological tradition in deepening our understanding both of ancient man and of humanism in general. I have italicized those of his remarks that may be particularly relevant today.

"For anyone today," wrote Welcker, "who wishes to pass judgment on the early period of the ancient peoples and on the later works that

6. Siegmann, *Literarische griechische Texte der Heidelberger Papyrussammlung*, pp. 21 f.
7. Reinhardt, "Vorschläge zum neuen Aeschylus," *Hermes*, LXXXV (1957), 12 ff.

refer to it, it is just as indispensable to develop a proper understanding and feeling for those early realities as it was in Winckelmann's time to discover beauty in art if one wished in that day, when something new was being said about marbles and documents—these historical sources that had long been available—to know what was actually being discussed. There were many who simply had no wish to learn; they ridiculed or even vilified the new idea that something they had never seen might be found in the ancient works. An old gentleman in Rome, who was then a young sculptor, has told me what a rage he and his young friends flew into over the young German (*quel giovine tedesco*) who had suddenly begun to cause a great stir in Rome. Their motto at the time was: *l'antico non vale un fico* (antiquity isn't worth a fig). But from the way the old man smiled at his former opinions one could only conclude that progress had been made since then. Between Berninesque art and a view of myths which excludes all ideal elements and considers only the material factor in accordance with the most prosaic rational concepts, often exaggerated to the point of caricature, so that the true nature even of an uncultured period ceases to be recognizable, the difference is perhaps not as great as might appear at first sight. But assuredly the comparison is apt to the extent that one must approach both the works of the later art and the myths of the earlier period with intelligence, sensibility, and understanding. *These qualities are engendered and molded by the objects themselves; but once the spark is struck, it is communicable. A time will come when the light which, not without merit, the few firstcomers held up to such objects will, if the great process of research is actively and conscientiously continued, be used with little effort by many: and when that happens, it will not be easy for anyone to deny that the light exists*" (pp. 7 f.).

VI. THE WORLD IN POSSESSION OF FIRE

From 'The Fire Kindler'

UNLESS THE texts come to light some day, we shall never be able to form a concrete idea of such lost literary works as the two tragedies *Prometheus Pyrphoros* and *Prometheus Lyomenos* and the satyric drama *Prometheus Pyrkaeus*. Even a credible reconstruction of the works themselves, of their structure, or of details that have not come down to us is out of the question. For where are we to derive a standard of credibility when we are dealing with something that surpasses all our calculations, with unrepeatable creations, with moments in the life of an artist, such "moments" as the *Pyrphoros*, the *Lyomenos*, the *Pyrkaeus*?

From the satyric drama *The Fire Kindler*, from a source that gives the full title of the play, we have only a single verse: "And linen-lint and long bands of raw flax."[1] This can refer only to the making of torches intended to burn for a long while. Such, no doubt, were Prometheus' instructions to the satyrs who on the vase paintings are shown dancing round him with torches [VIII, IX, Xa, XI]. They represent the original men, who, to judge by the vase shards from the Kabeirion of Thebes, were not conceived very differently from them [Xb]. Quite possibly the verse refers to the preparations for the torch races characteristic of certain of the great Athenian festivals—the Greater Panathenaia and the festivals of Prometheus and Hephaistos. In all

---

1. Apart from the Oxyrhynchus and Heidelberg fragments and Cicero's quotations, the English of the Aischylos fragments here quoted is from the translation of Herbert Weir Smyth (LCL). Here Nauck, fr. 206 (tr. Smyth, II, 453, fr. 115).
λινᾶ δέ, πίσσα κὠμολίνου μακροὶ τόνοι.

likelihood Prometheus was here establishing the ceremony of the *lampas, lampadedromia,* or *lampadephoria.* This presupposes that Prometheus had already brought the fire. But this he did in a very particular way—in a "hollow fennel-stalk," as we have heard from Hesiod —and so too he is represented in the vase paintings; his fire-bringing rod is distinguished from the torches of the satyrs [particularly XI]. He was not a *lampadephoros,* but the *pyrphoros,* and correspondingly the *lampadephoria* are never called *pyrphoria,* which would have been possible from a purely linguistic standpoint. The bringing of the fire to men was a unique act, with which, according to this play, the first torch race seems to have been associated, not as a repetition of Prometheus' act, but as a sacred action, which he inaugurated. Once there was fire on earth, man was provided with this possibility of imitating the heavenly fires and their circuit.

But both the satyrs and the first men had to learn how to handle fire. Another fragment quoted from one of the Prometheus plays of Aischylos, but not expressly from the *Pyrkaeus,* was thought to have belonged to a scene representing a lesson in fire kindling: "And do thou guard thee well lest a bubble strike thy face; for it is bitter, and deadly-scorching its vapors." [2]

But has this really to do with the kindling of fire? Does fire in flaring up form bubbles (*pémphix*) and dangerous vapors (*atmoí*)? Are these not rather instructions for operating a primitive smelting furnace such as we still find in use in Africa? [XVI] [3] This scene should probably be placed in the workshop—a smithy where iron is also pro-

2. Nauck, fr. 205 (tr. Smyth, II, 454, fr. 116, modified).
ἐξευλαβοῦ δὲ μή σε προσβάληι στόμα,
πέμφιξ· πικρὰ γὰρ κοὐ διὰ ζόης ἀτμοί.
3. René Gardi, *Der schwarze Hephaestus,* a collection of illustrations of the smiths of the Matakam in the Mandara Mountains of northern Cameroons and their primordial art of iron smelting.

duced—of Prometheus, who is instructing an apprentice. Or perhaps Epimetheus is the instructor and possibly the fragment is related to the Heidelberg fragment (see pp. 72 ff.).

With great probability, however, we can assign to the *Pyrkaeus* the following verse, cited without title or author but with the indication that it is spoken by Prometheus: "Like the goat, you'll mourn for your beard, you will!" [4] We also have a description of the scene. [5] A satyr, no doubt the chorus leader in the play, wishes to embrace and kiss Prometheus' acquisition, which is quite unknown to him. The Titan warns him.

The Oxyrhynchus Fragment

THE satyr's desire to kiss the fire leads us among the creatures who rejoice over Prometheus' gift. Is it the same chorus leader who, in the few legible and wholly intelligible lines of the Oxyrhynchus fragment, leads the chorus in a song with refrain? The members of the chorus are surely satyrs, for they think only of the nymphs whom they summon to the fire as though to a new-found spring. And in the presence of the fire, the satyrs and nymphs will do what they have always done at springs. "If the nymph hearken to me, I will pursue her by the firelight. I am trustful of the nymphs; they usher in the round to celebrate Prometheus' gift." [6]

---

4. Nauck, fr. 207 (tr. Smyth, II, 454, fr. 117).

> τράγος γένειον ἆρα πενθήσεις σύ γε.

5. Plutarch, *Moralia* 86 F.
6. See ch. v, n. 4.

> κλύουσ' ἐμοῦ δὲ ναΐδων τις παρ' ἑσ-
> τιοῦχον σέλας πολλὰ διώξεται.
> νύμφας δέ τοι πέποιθ' ἐγὼ
> στήσειν χόρους
> Προμηθέως δῶρον ὡς σεβούσας.

The last three lines are those that recur like a refrain. The following lines, which have been preserved only incompletely, are full of the glorification of Prometheus: he is the life-bringer (*pherésbios*) for mortals; he has hastened with his gift (*speusídōros*). The earth is inhabited not only by satyrs and nymphs but also by men, and the Titan comes to their help with his gift. The situation is that of the *Pyrkaeus:* the state of the world after the fire bringer has brought his gift, at which even the gods rejoice.

The Heidelberg Fragment

I N the Heidelberg fragment,[7] which consists of fifteen lines from the middle of a play and has neither beginning nor end, there are no satyrs; the chorus is made up of Titans. The following words can be read without difficulty: "he kindled the fire's light for mortals"[8] and, later on, "unfortunate blood kin,"[9] which can refer only to the Titans. According to Cicero,[10] these same words were spoken by the chained Prometheus in the *Prometheus Lyomenos:*

> *Titanum suboles, socia nostri sanguinis*
> (*Offspring of Titans, linked in blood to ours!*).

This would indicate that Aischylos himself or an imitator used a chorus of Titans elsewhere than in the *Lyomenos*. If it was Aischylos himself, it seems very unlikely that he would have done so in a play whose action follows the release of Prometheus, which the Titans witness in the

---

7. See ch. v, n. 6.   8. πυρὸς ἦψε φαὸς βροτοῖς.   9. δύσποτμοι ξυναίμονες.
10. *Tusculan Disputations* II 10 23 (tr. King, p. 171).

Lyomenos. What their strange kinsman did after his release can scarcely have been a source of great wonder to them. It seems more likely that their interest was aroused by the practice of his arts, if they were the *immediate* consequence of his theft of the fire, and later on by their consequences, his sufferings. The chorus of Titans may perfectly well have appeared a *second* time in the *Lyomenos.*

The novelty they are witnessing is the smithy with its far-echoing sound.[11] "It sings." What sings? The following seems to be an excellent reconstruction: "The brass resounds far and wide and sings so loud."[12] On the stage no doubt, as above in the second quotation, which has erroneously been assigned to the *Pyrkaeus,* stands the first smithy of the primeval world, set up by the fire bringer.

It would surely take us too far to lay stress on the difference between "brass" and "iron" in the language of the Attic dramatists. Their words for smith and the products of the smithy stem from the Bronze Age and referred originally to the ancient craft which was preserved by artists but not by the common artisans. In the Kabeirian sanctuary of Samothrace there was probably a primitive smelting furnace,[13] used for the manufacture of the iron rings which the initiates, as we shall learn below, wore in imitation of Prometheus. What matters here is not the metal but the atmosphere. In support of this contention I wish to cite a very vivid example from Africa. In quite the spirit of the

11. The reading χαλκοτυπει is to connect with χαλκοτύπος and χαλκοτυπεῖν, "black-smith" and "(to) forge." And the word certainly does not refer to the "forging" of Prometheus to his cliff. The situation and the atmosphere surrounding it are entirely different, above all, more cheerful. He is working on an ἄγαλμα, a statue, probably an ἄγαλμα παρθένου, the statue of a virgin.

12. χαλκὸς κτυπεῖ μα]κρᾶι τε μέλπε[ται βοᾶι.
By Reinhardt, *Hermes,* LXXXV (1957), 15. Some of his other reconstructions are based on the assumption that the fragment belongs to the *Pyrphoros,* and that this play follows the *Lyomenos;* the last assumption is surely false.

13. Kerényi, *Unwillkürliche Kunstreisen,* p. 115.

traveler to Africa referred to above,[14] a great writer [15] describes the atmosphere of just such a primordial workshop from her own experience:

". . . the Native world was drawn to the forge by its song. The treble, sprightly, monotonous, and surprising rhythm of the blacksmith's work has a mythical force. It is so virile that it appals and melts the women's hearts, it is straight and unaffected and tells the truth and nothing but the truth. Sometimes it is very outspoken. It has an excess of strength and is gay as well as strong, it is obliging to you and does great things for you, willingly, as in play. The Natives, who love rhythm, collected by Pooran Singh's hut and felt at their ease. According to an ancient Nordic law a man was not held responsible for what he had said in a forge. The tongues were loosened in Africa as well in the blacksmith's shop, and the talk flowed freely; audacious fancies were set forth to the inspiring hammer-song." And now, an exact parallel to the reconstructed line of the fragment: "In Pooran Singh's blacksmith's shop the hammer *sang* to you what you wanted to hear, as if it was giving voice to your own heart."

The appearance of *Ga mater*, Mother Earth, under whose protection Prometheus seems to have placed himself, is also a certainty in the fragment. She was, in particular, the mother of the ancestors of the Athenians, the natives of Attica: [16] everything that happened in this tragedy could have taken place in Attica before the punishment of Prometheus, even if he had been destined to suffer for thirty thousand years as was forecast in the *Pyrphoros*—which, however, did not come to pass. Did the events leading to the punishment occur in the play,

14. Note 3.
15. Karen Blixen (pseud. Isak Dinesen), *Out of Africa*, pp. 311 and 312 (Penguin edn., p. 334).
16. Kerényi, *Gods*, p. 210.

and was this play the *Pyrphoros*? Both are possible and even probable, but one cannot say for certain. Here we have arrived at the limit of the knowable, and here we must remain for a moment, at least long enough to dispose of an apparent difficulty in connection with the position of the *Pyrphoros*.

The Position of the 'Pyrphoros'

T H E subject matter and position of the two lost tragedies of the trilogy and their relation to the preserved *Prometheus Desmotes* would seem to be made clear by their titles, which suggest that the *Pyrphoros* must have directly preceded the *Desmotes*, while the *Lyomenos* must have followed it. And this was assuredly the case.

In the *Desmotes*, Prometheus, chained to the cliff, speaks of the term of his sufferings in words that are moving but not wholly clear (93–95):

> See in what tortures I must struggle
> through countless years of time.[17]

The word *myrietḗs*, here translated as "countless years," also has the meaning of "ten thousand years." Prometheus is only at the beginning of his torments; he speaks of them in the future as still to come. The Greek makes it clear that he has in mind a fixed period of time. He has no need to state its exact length—and this for several reasons: the audience already knows the allotted time of his punishment; in this

---

17. The English of the passages quoted from Aischylos' *Prometheus Bound* is, with one exception, the translation of Edith Hamilton in *Three Greek Plays;* here, p. 100. The line numbering is that of the OCT edn.

δέρχθηθ' οἴαις αἰκίαισιν
διακναιόμενος τὸν μυριετῆ
χρόνον ἀθλεύσω.

situation he naturally inclines to exaggeration; he nourishes the hope of being released before the allotted time has elapsed. And this indeed is what happens—he will be released in the thirteenth generation after Io, who is soon to appear on the stage. It is Prometheus himself who predicts this to Io, this time with precision (774).

In order to remedy the imprecision of the first prophecy, an ancient or Byzantine commentator [18] informs the reader: "He (the poet) says in the *Pyrphoros* that he was chained for thirty thousand years." The figure also occurs in Empedokles,[19] who tells us that the divine spirits (*daimones*) who have been guilty of bloodshed are condemned to wander about the earth for thrice ten thousand years in divers shapes. This seems to have been the standard term of punishment for Titans. However, the line as it stands in the scholium cannot have occurred in the *Pyrphoros,* particularly not if this play *followed* the *Lyomenos.* For in that case every member of the audience would have been aware that the Titan, as he had prophesied to Io, would be liberated by one of her descendants, in the thirteenth generation, before expiration of his full term. As we have already suggested, it is only if the *Pyrphoros* was the first play of the trilogy that any such statement could have occurred, probably in the final scene, and then not in that form or in the form of a prophecy but as a decree to the effect that Prometheus must go into exile for thirty thousand years and there be chained.[20] There can scarcely be doubt that in the *Pyrphoros* Prometheus brought the fire, and we shall have to say a few words about this before interpreting the *Desmotes.*

18. Scholium on τρεῖς μυριάδας δεδέσθαι αὐτόν.
19. Diels, fr. 115 6 (an English version in Freeman, p. 65).
20. The "quotation" is limited to τρεῖς μυριάδας, or more likely: εἰς τρεῖς μυριάδας. Only the meaning of the word δεδέσθαι can be ascribed to Aischylos. The perfect tense shows that the word itself was inserted by the commentator.

VII. THE FIRE STEALER

The Deficient Nature of the Thief

AFTER all the beings on earth—including the satyrs and nymphs —had been cheered by the gift of fire, events took a tragic turn. The tradition does not tell us exactly what happened, and reconstruction is impossible. The most we can do is to derive the general tenor of the events from the mythologem as a whole: Prometheus had made common cause with men; by their side he is involved in new weaknesses and difficulties. Our ideas on the subject must inevitably hover in the sphere of possibilities and probabilities until we come into possession of a coherent text comparable to the *Theogony* and the *Works and Days*.

The theft of the fire—because it is theft—characterizes the thief as one whose existence is inherently deficient. Fire was not essential to Hermes and he did not steal it, but discovered it by his own inventiveness, in his own mind as it were—so the great Homeric hymn tells us. To Hephaistos, on the other hand, fire was so essential that his name is even used to designate it. He *has* fire, and for this reason the human mode of life, which would be impossible without it, can be said to have begun with him—the Homeric hymn to Hephaistos says just this. His gift, however, was not the expression of any deficiency, but of his wealth: to men, who previously had been living like beasts in mountain caves, he brought not fire but his works and the art of fashioning them [1]—Prometheus also attempted to do this, but his efforts were tragically frustrated by his punishment. Neither Hephaistos nor

1. Homeric Hymn XX 4 (ed. Allen).

Hermes had any need to steal fire. The darkness of Prometheus signifies precisely the deficiency of one who needs fire in order to achieve a
more perfect form of being. In obtaining this higher form of being for
man, Prometheus shows himself to be man's double, an eternal image
of man's basically imperfect form of being.

Aischylos evokes this eternal image as the god Prometheus, bene-
factor of mankind, and in his eternalized form of being—which represents a timeless potentiality quite independent of its fulfillment—he
emphasizes the basic traits of the human mode of existence. He does so
in the second and third tragedies of the trilogy, dealing primarily with
two such traits which we shall soon consider. These two plays also
throw light on the essential trait which—to judge by the title—was the
theme of the first tragedy.

Pyrphoros—Fire Bringer—simply identifies Prometheus as the
bringer of fire, without branding him as a sinner. Prometheus had to
carry his fire a long way, particularly if he set up his smithy in Attica.
That is all that is stressed here. Of course the acquisition of fire was a
theft for Aischylos just as it was for Hesiod. In the *Desmotes* he describes the theft in the same terms as Hesiod. However, the title given
to the play either by the poet himself or by others on the strength of the
impression it made on them suggests that no condemnation of Prometheus is contained in this first tragedy. And yet the terrible punishment,
the thirty thousand years of torture decreed at the end of this same
play, ensued. We can only conclude that the *Pyrphoros* lays the
foundation for the sufferings we shall witness at the very beginning
of the second play, showing how man as typified by Prometheus is
compelled to do wrong, so that inevitable wrongdoing is a fundamental
trait of his existence.

The Inevitable Theft

T H E crime was inevitable because without fire mankind would have perished—this was the design of Zeus, as we are expressly told in *Desmotes* (232)—and this inevitable act was a crime, because power over fire—as over all things that "grow" and are not produced by man —was the prerogative of the ruler of the world. This juridical situation —Zeus in the right, man in the wrong—is the presupposition of the *Desmotes*. Hesiod, in describing the details of this necessary wrong-doing—the theft of the fire—tells us that Zeus "did not give" fire to men: "From that time he was always mindful of the trick, and would not give the power of unwearying fire to the wretched race of mortal men . . . ," [2] or again: "Therefore he planned sorrow and mischief against men. He hid fire. . . ." [3]

Thereupon Prometheus "stole" the fire, deceiving Zeus with the trick of a master thief: what he secretly stole he carried away "in the hollow of the narthex (giant fennel) stalk," [4] in the *Theogony* as well as in *Works and Days*.

> *I hunted out the secret source of fire.*
> *I filled a fennel-stalk therewith,* [5]

says Prometheus in *Desmotes* (108–9), and the word "source" recalls the song of the satyrs in the Oxyrhynchus fragment.

2. *Theogony* 562 (tr. Evelyn-White, p. 121).
3. *Works and Days* 50 (tr. ibid., pp. 5, 7).   4. ἐν κοίλωι νάρθηκι.
5. ναρθηκοπλήρωτον δὲ θηρῶμαι πυρός
   πηγὴν κλοπαίαν.

A true Promethean trick. It no doubt accounts for the custom of
keeping and carrying fire in this way, which has survived down to
modern times on some of the Greek Islands, just as conversely the
custom explains the trick: a sacred practice which men had been compelled to observe from time immemorial.[6] Prometheus seems to have
carried the fire a long way. Speaking of Prometheus' speech to the
chorus of Titans in the *Lyomenos*, Cicero refers to the theft of fire as
furtum Lemnium, "the theft of Lemnos."[7] This suggests that Aischylos
situated the event on the distant island of Lemnos in the Thracian Sea.
The allusion was formerly thought to mark a difference between the
tragic poet and the Hesiodic tradition. For, according to *Works and
Days* (51), Prometheus stole the fire from Zeus. Later sources,[8] which
may—we do not know—have been based on the lost tragedies of
Aischylos, tell us how Prometheus made his way by stealth to the fire
of Zeus—presumably the hearth fire of the palace of the gods on
Olympos. He took an ember and hid it in the narthex stalk, which he
waved in the air to keep the fire burning. And thus he journeyed, as
though flying, to the abode of men, possibly to Lemnos. According to
another, still later version,[9] Prometheus reached the wheel of the sun
and tore a brand from it. The island of Lemnos, as we know, possesses
a kind of volcano: the fiery crater of Mosychlos on the north side of
the island where Hephaistos had his sanctuary and his city of He-
phaistias. The belief inevitably arose that Prometheus may simply

6. The marrow of the narthex, the giant fennel, *Ferula communis,* served also
as tinder, as Walter Kraus points out in his article "Prometheus," in Pauly-Wissowa,
RE, ser. 2, XLV, col. 694. Documentation concerning the fire custom of the Greek
Islands appears already in Welcker, *Die Aeschylische Trilogie,* p. 8, and in Frazer's
note to Apollodoros, *Library* I 52.   7. Cicero, *Tusc.* II 10 23 (tr. King, p. 171).
8. E.g., Hyginus, *Astronomica* II 15 (ed. Bunte, p. 53).
9. Scholium on Virgil's sixth Eclogue (42). Both versions in Kerényi, *Gods,* p.
216. All sources in Kraus, col. 694. For Prometheus in art, see Lothar Eckhart in Pauly-
Wissowa, *RE,* ser. 2, XLV, cols. 702–30.

have stolen the fire from Hephaistos' smithy and of this too we find artistic representations [IIb, III].

But this does not seem to have been the meaning of the "theft of Lemnos," not at least for Aischylos, as can be seen from a passage at the very beginning of the *Desmotes*. The subterranean gases of Mosychlos had, after all, to be ignited. Hephaistos worked in the depths of the earth and, as we know from the Iliad (XVIII 402), of the sea. As the play opens Hephaistos appears to chain Prometheus to the cliff as Zeus has commanded. He does so with the utmost reluctance. Kratos, the bailiff of Zeus, has to tell him expressly that it was his *anthos,* his "flower," a plant belonging to him, that Prometheus had filched and handed on to men (7). This does not give us the impression that Hephaistos felt robbed. If—in accordance with the representations on the late sarcophagi (IIa, III; IIb)—the Titan had broken into Hephaistos' workshop, the god assuredly would have felt wronged. No, just as in Hesiod, the fire originates with Zeus, and from Olympos it first came to Lemnos—like Hephaistos himself, who, according to the Iliad (I 592–94), was hurled from Olympos to Lemnos. In the *Pyrphoros* as well, Aischylos seems to have followed this tradition of the *furtum Lemnium,* and the scene of the tragedy may actually have been the remote island of the Kabeiroi.[10]

The people of Lemnos venerated the Kabeiroi as the original divine inhabitants of the island, its "first men." They were also regarded as sons of Hephaistos, a genealogy that may well have been combined with the Homeric mythologem in which Hephaistos was flung down upon Lemnos. According to a Lemnian tradition, it was the island itself that gave birth to the eldest of the Kabeiroi, the first man.[11] The

10. The sea between the island and the mainland argues against Attica.
11. Hippolytos, *Refutatio* V 7 4 (cf. Legge, I, 122).

Lemnian Kabeiroi were termed *Karkinoi*, "Crabs": [12] the word brings to mind a swarming population of primordial beings and also suggests the tongs used in primitive smithies. The legend of how the Kabeiroi emigrated in consequence of the hostility of the Lemnian women suggests that they were virile primordial gods.[13] All this does not settle the question of the origin of the purloined fire, and is mentioned only by way of enriching our picture. In his trilogy of the *Argonauts*, Aischylos devotes a special tragedy, the *Kabeiroi*, to the return of the primordial Lemnians to their island. This was a tragedy of Dionysian exuberance; the wine flows so freely that there are not enough barrels to hold it, and the heroic followers of Jason appear on the stage reeling drunk. Drunken gods and heroes are highly unusual in Greek drama, to us almost unthinkable, and the strangeness of their occurrence here was remarked even in antiquity.[14] Still, one cannot help wondering how much more that is unthinkable, though at bottom perfectly natural, may lie buried beneath a mere title such as *The Firebringer*.

12. Gloss of Hesychios.   13. Kerényi, *Heroes*, p. 255.
14. Athenaios, *The Deipnosophists* 428 f (cf. LCL edn., IV, 442–43).

VIII. THE 'PROMETHEUS BOUND'

Cosmogonic Tragedy

T H E *Prometheus Bound* is for us *the* Prometheus tragedy, indeed *the* poem concerning Prometheus, the only work wholly devoted to Prometheus that has come down to us from antiquity. But this tragedy is unique also for another reason: it does not deal with heroes, like the other tragedies known to us, but with cosmogony, taken in the Greek sense as the founding of the world. It presupposes the decisive founding act of Zeus, the defeat of the Titans—but this, too, had been accomplished with the help of Prometheus (218). This first founding act establishes a juridical situation—*dikē* as the common measure for gods and men (29-30)—intended to bring about the doom of the human race (233). *Prometheus Pyrphoros,* the first tragedy in Aischylos' Prometheus trilogy, relates how Prometheus attenuated this situation and saved the human race. The second tragedy, *Prometheus Desmotes,* or *Prometheus Bound,* discloses the state of affairs under the new rule of Zeus (35, 96, 144, 310) and the other Olympians (955). The new order, however, is represented not as secured for all time but as subject to further cosmogonic developments. What gives this drama movement and tension is the possibility of a founding that will surpass Zeus and the Olympians—just as the age of the Titans was surpassed by the founding acts of Zeus. It is only the third tragedy, *Prometheus Lyomenos,* that eliminates this threat and leads to the firmly established, definitively ordered world in which we live.

The Rule of Zeus

W H A T moves us from the very beginning of the second tragedy is its picture of this order in which Zeus holds absolute power. Kratos, personified Force, appears on the stage, dragging Prometheus; they are accompanied by Hephaistos and the silent Violence (Greek, Bia). Kratos describes the new order with its unbending, all-encompassing new laws (150), and sums up the situation in line 50: "No one is free but Zeus." [1] He alone stands above the laws, his is the *nomos*, the Law. These are the words of a being who has no existence except as an agent of an abstract, unfeeling, omnipotent order. By comparison, an elemental being like Hephaistos seems soft. Two aspects of man's environment are contrasted: Kratos represents the unyielding hardness of the world that surrounds us on all sides, while the elemental beings who participate in the tragedy betoken its kinship with us and friendliness.

Hephaistos professes both kinship and friendliness toward Prometheus. He shrinks back from binding (14–15 and 36–39)

> *a god, a kinsman, to this stormy crag.*

KRATOS: *Well, then, why this delay and foolish talk?*
A god whom gods hate is abominable.

HEPHAISTOS: *The tie of blood has a strange power,*
and old acquaintance too.

And after driving a wedge through Prometheus' breast (66–69):

1. The quotations in this chapter and those following are chiefly from the Hamilton tr. of *Prometheus Bound*. They are sometimes slightly modified to suit the context.

HEPHAISTOS: *Alas, Prometheus, I grieve for your pain.*

KRATOS: *You shirk your task and grieve for those Zeus hates?*
Take care; you may need pity for yourself.

HEPHAISTOS: *You see a sight eyes should not look upon.*

Thus at the very outset we behold a *théama dysthéaton*, a "sight that can scarcely be borne," and we look upon it up to the very end of the play when Prometheus is cast down into the depths of Tartaros. This is not a mere spectacle devised to entertain an audience with shivers of horror but a significant picture of the order introduced by Zeus, in which the old elements are governed by the new laws.

Prometheus and the Elements

HANGING in torment from the cliff to which he is riven and chained, Prometheus recalls Hera hanging down from heaven with two anvils fastened to her feet (Iliad XV 18–21), a situation befitting the moonlike goddess and another image one can hardly bear to look upon. But Prometheus wants to be seen. He calls upon the elements, for they are his kin, to whom he is bound by a relationship unique in Greek literature. It is an intimate and eminently human kinship and friendliness with the elements, such as we otherwise find only in Hölderlin. And nowhere else in Greek poetry do we perceive so Hölderlinian a note as in the following lines (88–93):

PROMETHEUS: *O air of heaven and swift-winged winds,*
O running river waters,
O never-numbered laughter of sea waves,
Earth, mother of all, Eye of the sun, all seeing,
on you I call.
Behold what I, a god, endure from gods.
See. . . .

But this passage also expresses the particularly Greek significance of Aischylos' picture of the order of Zeus. Prometheus calls in as witnesses the sacred elements and the sun, the supreme witness. His display of his torment serves to enhance the imagery, but it does not, like that of Goethe's Prometheus, spring from personal pride or arrogance. This is the cry of a Greek when he is persecuted unjustly: *martýromai* —"You who have seen, I summon you as witnesses." Here we have the first denunciation of an injustice before a court. Already Prometheus is suffering unspeakable torments, as Hephaistos himself laments while driving the wedge through Prometheus' breast in obedience to the higher power. But it is nothing beside the intolerable pain inflicted later on by the eagle which will devour his liver in the third tragedy. In the present play there is no mention of this. What Prometheus bemoans here is above all the disgrace (93–95):

See in what shameful tortures I must struggle
through countless years of time.

And he continues:

This shame, these bonds, are put upon me
by the new ruler of the gods.

The less emotional but no less shattering name for it is injustice. It rings out powerfully in the mouth of Prometheus, when in the last scene, struck down by Zeus' thunderbolt, he vanishes in Tartaros (1091–93):

> O holy Mother Earth, O air and sun,
> behold me. I am wronged.[2]

'In Excess of Justice'

AISCHYLOS does not, like Hesiod, explain that Zeus had denied men fire as punishment for a previous crime of Prometheus. According to the dramatist, the basis of the denial is "justice," *díkē*, the measure fixed by Zeus for gods and men. Hephaistos makes this clear at the beginning of the tragedy (29–30):

> A god yourself, you did not dread God's anger,
> but gave to mortals honor in excess of justice. . . .

This "in excess of justice," *péra díkēs*, seems to indicate that the punishment is just. But Aischylos' meaning is not as simple as all that. Let us consider the parallel words of the Titan, which imply no desire to change the fact and its relation to the order of Zeus. They are addressed to the daughters of Okeanos, who form the chorus (119–23):

> Look at me then, in chains, a god who failed,
> the enemy of Zeus, whom all gods hate,
> all that go in and out of Zeus' hall.
> The reason is that I loved men too well.

---

2. ὦ μητρὸς ἐμῆς σέβας, ὦ πάντων
αἰθὴρ κοινὸν φάος εἱλίσσων
ἐσορᾷς μ' ὡς ἔκδικα πάσχω.

The counterpart to "in excess of justice," *péra díkēs*, is here, in the mouth of Prometheus, too much love, too much friendship for men [3] —this, too, an "excess." And suddenly it becomes clear that the order to which this measure belongs is to blame for the sufferings of Prometheus, who has done nothing more than men are compelled to do. He put himself in our place—the place of men—and his actions and sufferings were the inevitable consequence. Our reflections about a possible *Pyrphoros* have indicated as much. And now it is perfectly clear: because his actions and sufferings resulted from his putting himself in the position of man, the source of his suffering is injustice.

The Zeus World and Human Existence

T H E world of Zeus is the real world in which man is compelled to live. Though at this stage it is not yet fully consolidated, this is the order represented in *Prometheus Bound,* where, in a way unparalleled in the history of Greek thought, it is called into question on the strength of Prometheus' suffering and, as we shall soon see, of his knowledge. The *mythológos* and tragic poet proves to be bolder than the philosophers. He recognizes the limit against which human existence must necessarily rebel as an unalterable fact of the existing world. Rebel—there is the source of a suffering peculiar to human existence: the suffering of injustice. Man has his bodily sufferings that he shares with the animals. The existential significance of these is dealt with in the last tragedy, the *Lyomenos.* But though man suffers like the beasts, his special mode of existence requires him to *suffer with a sense of injustice.* The animals, whose existence in pleasure and pain is in perfect

3. διὰ τὴν λίαν φιλότητα βρότων.

harmony with the order of Zeus, feel no such sense of injustice. Prometheus loved mankind. He could not do otherwise; that was his nature. He brought fire, the possession of which is denied the animals. The animals live without fire—that is the very nature of animal existence. Thus it was Prometheus who made human existence *human:* man remained vulnerable, suffering, mortal like the animals, but he did not remain submissive like the animals. Liberated, he was still chained and punished; this was the existence to which Prometheus raised men. For as soon as man is man, as soon as he appears as a being *sui generis*—and this is the case in the mythologem of Prometheus, who with his nature, his actions, and his sufferings expresses human existence—lack of fire becomes a deficiency that must be remedied: man becomes *unable* to submit. And the sufferings that spring from unsubmissiveness are special sufferings that exceed those of the animals—they become, in a sense, punishments. At first they are incomprehensible and nameless, and so they remain until the order to which man cannot submit, as an animal does, is related to a higher order subsisting in itself, independently of the world; until the human mind conceives of an ideal order of justice.

The Suffering of Prometheus

F O R Prometheus, too, his suffering is at first nameless, inevitable, and incomprehensible (106–8):

> *But silence is intolerable here.*
> *So too is speech.*
> *I am fast bound, I must endure.*
> *I gave to mortals gifts. . . .*

His fate is an incommensurable consequence of a mistake committed with a clear conscience—thus it has a character of existential suffering. And because it is embedded in his very existence, there is no help for it. This hopelessness is expressed in such words as these, spoken by Prometheus to the chorus (199–200):

> *To speak is pain, but silence too is pain,*
> *and everywhere is wretchedness.*

And so Prometheus proclaims his suffering to the elements. When Io appears and asks him (620):

> *Did you do wrong?*
> *Is this your punishment?*[4]

he does not reply. And how indeed could this persecuted maiden in the shape of a heifer, who suffers and displays the absolute defenselessness of woman in the order of Zeus, bear to hear of the defenseless suffering that is the lot of mankind. For men are exposed—Prometheus says as much in the above-cited last words of the tragedy—to *injustice*. Once Hephaistos, the submissive elemental god, has declared the existing order to be an order of justice, *dikē*, and so evoked the *idea* of *dikē*, a higher, ideal, self-subsisting order of justice, the logical corollary—injustice—was only to be expected. Once the word "justice" is spoken in our world order, the word "injustice" comes to mind in connection with all incomprehensible, nameless suffering. This is the *special* suffering that comes with human existence itself: not only to be doomed to suffering in an order which in all other respects strikes our mortal

---

4. ποινὰς δὲ ποίων ἀμπλακημάτων τίνεις;

eyes as admirably conceived but, on top of all this other inevitable suffering, to suffer injustice. That is man's punishment for being a man.

Aischylos distinguishes Prometheus' knowledge of destiny from the suffering induced in him by his knowledge of injustice. Though a god, he shares this suffering with man. And since he is a god, a helper and fellow founder beside the king of the gods, he also experiences his suffering as a disgrace. He stands before us as an image of injustice— and of offended divine pride. The young Goethe in his human situation put himself in the place of the gods, as though divine rank were man's due. For Aischylos the Greek, Prometheus as a god takes the standpoint of man. He suffers in his own sphere, humanity, whose advocate and eternal symbol he is, and does not set himself up as a countergod. As a god, he has knowledge of Fate; indeed, because he is the son of a goddess versed in the lore of the future his knowledge of things to come exceeds even that of Zeus. This is not the "crooked," devious knowledge known to us from Hesiod. Kratos, it is true, is justified in his mockery (85–87):

> *Forethought your name means, falsely named.*
> *Forethought you lack and need now for yourself*
> *if you would slip through fetters wrought like these.*

No more than mankind can Prometheus escape from the fetters of the Zeus world. His knowledge of Fate is powerless against the fundamental facts of human existence which he, the prototype, is first to suffer: bondage, pain, and the smart of injustice. It is no help to him against his present suffering, but it strengthens him for the future (102–5):

Nothing, no pang of pain
that I did not foresee.
Bear without struggle what must be.
Necessity is strong and ends our strife.
But silence is intolerable here.
So too is speech. . . .

Thus the present, of which he can neither speak nor keep silent, is distinguished from that other knowledge, the knowledge—in which Prometheus remains superior even to the king of the gods, who does not possess it—that possibly this order will one day be surpassed.

IX. PROMETHEUS THE KNOWING ONE

The Two Threads of the Tragedy

THE TWO THREADS from which this tragedy is spun are on the one hand Prometheus' suffering, his punishment for taking the standpoint of man, and on the other hand his secret knowledge. We have seen that the suffering which dominates the whole play—the second in the trilogy—is the moral suffering fundamental to human existence. It remains for us to examine the second thread, Prometheus' knowledge as it appears in Aischylos. Like Hesiod, the dramatic poet regarded guile as the characteristic and original attribute of Prometheus. We are told how, with the help of this quality, he even helped Zeus to defeat Kronos and the Titans (219–21). Quite possibly this is a reference to an event recorded in the *Titanomachia*. But if the messenger of the Titans sided with the future king of the gods, it was surely because he foresaw that the victorious order would be founded not by the wild power of the Titans but by Zeus with the help of Promethean guile (213):

> *That neither violence nor strength of arm*
> *but only subtle craft could win.*

And Zeus lacked both the deviousness of Prometheus and his knowledge, the prescience he inherited from his mother.

Zeus, the Father

THE triumph of Zeus ushered in an order in which the father was the sole ruler and lawgiver. This is clear from the cosmogonic happenings that Aischylos dramatizes, and it is also stated expressly. When Hephaistos refers to his friendly kinship with Prometheus, Kratos replies (40):

> *And so say I—but don't you think*
> *that disobedience to the Father's words*
> *might have still stranger power?*

But in Greek mythology Hephaistos was known as his *mother's* son. He is identified as such in the famous scene from the Iliad (I 571–600) and in Hesiod's *Theogony* (927) he is specifically said to be a son only of Hera and not of Zeus. His deference to the paternal discipline in the *Prometheus Bound* is a clear allusion to the prevailing father right. As for Hermes, he submits with shameless cynicism and shares in the power. His words of mockery hardly suggest sincere filial devotion, but merely subjection to the law of the father (968–69):

> *Better no doubt to be slave to a rock*
> *than be the Father's trusted herald.*

And the appearance of Io, reduced to the defenselessness of womanhood, also throws a glaring light on the radically patriarchal character of the new order.

Okeanos and His Daughters

FRIENDLY kinship, the softer aspect of the environment, is present but not dominant in Hephaistos. It comes to Prometheus in the form of winged, primordial feminine beings: the daughters of Okeanos, the sea nymphs. At first he seems frightened at their approach (114–19):

> *But what is here? What comes?*
> *What sound, what fragrance, brushed me with faint wings,*
> *of deities or mortals or of both?*
> *Has someone found a way to this far peak*
> *to view my agony? What else?*
> *Look at me, an unlucky god in chains. . . .*

And then, still more frightened, for it may be the eagle that is coming (124–27):

> *Oh, birds are moving near me. The air murmurs*
> *with swift and sweeping wings.*
> *Whatever comes to me is terrible.*

But thereupon the appeasing song of the daughters of Okeanos (128–35):

> *Oh, be not terrified, for friends are here,*
> *each eager to be first,*
> *on swift wings flying to your rock.*
> *I prayed my father long*
> *before he let me come.*
> *The rushing winds have sped me on.*
> *A noise of ringing brass went through the sea-caves,*
> *and for all a maiden's fears it drove me forth,*
> *so swift, I did not put my sandals on,*
> *but in my winged car I came to you.*

The father who wished to restrain his daughters was Okeanos, according to Homer the oldest of the gods: the masculine form of the primordial element whose feminine manifestations are the sea nymphs. Soon he too appears on a miraculous bird, just as his daughters have appeared in a miraculous chariot. He too is driven by a sympathy born of kinship (288–90):

> *Now you must know, I'm grieved at your misfortunes.*
> *Of course I must be, I'm your kinsman.*

But what a difference in attitude between Okeanos and Prometheus and between father and daughters!

The epiphany of a primordial element submissive to the new world order was needed to bring out the conciliatory attitude of the all-sustaining pillars of nature—Okeanos was one of these in the Greek view of the world—and the contrasting human stubbornness of Prometheus. Against this background, his Titanic, human character stands out sharply. But in contrast with the eager sympathy of the sea nymphs, who cling to Prometheus in his weakness, prepared to share his doom, the submissiveness of Okeanos, this god of primeval strength, strikes one as cowardly masculine opportunism. It is Prometheus who has introduced all these complex ambiguities into the world order by knowingly taking upon himself the lot of man: to suffer and to suffer injustice. For, trusting in his knowledge, Prometheus despises Father Okeanos, who offers him peace with the king of the gods.

The Knowledge of Prometheus

WHAT Prometheus knows is a secret. He speaks of it only in hints and only to his fellow sufferers, the sea nymphs and the suffering Io. But as though by chance, the chorus, no sooner arrived, brings up the subject of the secret (160–67):

> *What god so hard of heart to look on these things gladly?*
> *Who, but Zeus only, would not suffer with you?*
> *He is malignant always and his mind*
> *unbending. All the sons of heaven*
> *he drives beneath his yoke.*
> *Nor will he make an end*
> *until his heart is sated or until*
> *someone, somehow, shall seize his sovereignty—*
> *if that could be.*

And now that this possibility—the possibility that the power may some day be wrested from Zeus—has been stated, Prometheus strikes the second keynote of the tragedy, his knowledge of a future redemption (168–70):

> *And yet—and yet—all tortured though I am,*
> *fast fettered here,*
> *he shall have need of me, the lord of heaven. . . .*

And in reply to the fearful doubts of the chorus (189–95):

> *I know that he is savage.*
> *He keeps his righteousness at home.*
> *But yet some time he shall be mild of mood,*
> *when he is broken.*
> *He will smooth his stubborn temper,*
> *and run to meet me.*
> *Then peace will come and love between us two.*

But with all this Prometheus does not reveal his secret. He cradles himself in the hope he weaves from his knowledge of the secret, so showing how very human he is. At the end of the third tragedy, the *Lyomenos,* the spectator will see for himself that the pact of friendship with Zeus will turn out to be something quite different from what Prometheus now hopes. He himself tells the sea nymphs how he has "cured" poor mortals of the fear of death (250):

> *Blind hopes I caused to dwell in them.*

Only then do the daughters of Okeanos learn that, in addition to this gift befitting mankind, Prometheus has also given them fire, to which only the gods are entitled. Hence the terror of the chorus (255–75):

CHORUS: *And now the creatures of a day*
have flaming fire?

PROMETHEUS: *Yes, and learn many crafts therefrom.*

CHORUS: *For deeds like these Zeus holds you guilty?*

PROMETHEUS: *And tortures me with never ease from pain.*

CHORUS: *Is no end to your tortures set before you?*

PROMETHEUS: *None other except when it pleases him.*

CHORUS: *It pleases him? What hope there? You must see*
you missed your mark. I tell you this with pain
to give you pain.
But let that pass. Seek your deliverance.

PROMETHEUS: *Your feet are free.*
Chains bind mine fast.
Advice is easy for the fortunate.
All that has come I knew full well.

Of my own will I shot the arrow that fell short,
of my own will.
Nothing do I deny.
I helped men and found trouble for myself.
I knew—and yet not all.
I did not think to waste away
hung high in air upon a lonely rock.
But now, I pray you, no more pity
for what I suffer here. Come, leave your car,
and learn the fate that steals upon me. . . .

This avowal of the Titan that he gladly erred and made trouble for himself for the benefit of men—that is, knowingly—confirms our seemingly so bold interpretation of the destiny of Prometheus as self-chosen human existence. He knew that to suffer punishment was implicit in the human condition; what he did not know was the terrible punishment Zeus had devised for him. And this again is typical of the human lot: the unexpected is not *what* will befall but *how* it will befall.

Mother Themis

T H E appearance of Father Okeanos, the peaceable soul who would like to save the world from a new upheaval, prevents Prometheus from revealing anything more about his secret. But he has at least named the source of the strange, mysterious knowledge which he so humanly spins out into a dazzling hope: the Mother.

In the Oxyrhynchus fragment the mother of the Titans is mentioned as *Ga mater*, "Mother Earth." Prometheus also calls her by another name, Chthon (207), mother of the first great Titans. As his own mother he mentions Themis (211), and it is hard to decide whether the next line

> *Earth whose form is one, whose name is many* [1]

was added by Aischylos himself, as though in parentheses to emphasize the unity of the great maternal deity amid her many aspects, or was inserted by someone else. Critics have been far too much inclined to regard this *mythológos* as the mere theologian of a patriarchal religion. But if in *his* mythologem he selected, as mother of Prometheus, Themis, who is neither "crooked" nor "devious" but a "straight counselor" (18), he was *bound* to stress her identity with the Titan mother of another tradition, a trace of which is preserved perhaps in the Oxyrhynchus papyrus. In the tradition which Hesiod and Aischylos himself also follow, Themis is a daughter of the Earth Mother Gaia, a Titaness (874). Her name expresses the regularity of nature, the peaceful law shared by all its creatures. This lawfulness is called *thémis.* Preceding Apollo—*Loxias,* the "Oblique One"—she was the great oracle goddess of Delphi, as was also Gaia.

The Horai who pass as her daughters also throw light on the nature of Themis. These three goddesses disclose two aspects, corresponding no doubt to two aspects of their mother. In Athens, they bore the names of Thallo, Auxo, Karpo, from sprouting, growing, ripening, and they were scarcely distinguishable from the three Graces.[2] In Hesiod,[3] they bore the names Legality, Justice, Peace: Eunomia, Dike, Eirene. *Horai* means periods of time, rhythmic periods of the world's unfolding. Developing into symbols of an ideal—lawful, just, peaceful

---

1. καὶ Γαῖα, πολλῶν ὀνομάτων μορφὴ μία.
2. Pausanias IX 35 2; Hyginus, *Fabulae* 183 (ed. Schmidt, p. 36).
3. *Theogony* 902.

—world order, they bear witness to the deep-rooted belief that a just order has its natural foundation in Themis, the earthly maternal principle, which protects and brings forth growth and fruit.

A knowledge of time and growth is an attribute of the oracle goddess and the secret that Prometheus has from her relates—as we shall soon see—to something that strives to grow, to ripen in time, and to which Zeus himself as a father is subordinate: for it is through such growth in time, through the forthcoming marriage, that he *becomes* the father. According to the prevailing mythological tradition, according to Hesiod and Pindar,[4] it was with Themis herself that Zeus celebrated the world-founding marriage that was to consolidate the world order and bring universal contentment. But the possibility of such a marriage he owed to Prometheus, who in the battle against the Titans had won his mother over to the side of Zeus. Was this too in the *Titanomachia?* At all events Prometheus expresses the thought in Aischylos (218–20):

> *The best then left me was to stand with Zeus*
> *in all good will, my mother with me. . . .*

This was not a marriage—or not yet. But did it, in the *Titanomachia,* for example, lead to a marriage between the great goddess and the victorious king of the gods? Did Aischylos follow the old mythological epic more closely than anyone has ever ventured to suppose and then keep silent throughout the trilogy concerning the cosmogonic marriage of Themis and Zeus? His mythologem no longer forms a whole for us. In this tragedy, it is certain, Themis has closer ties with Prometheus, her son, than with Zeus. How otherwise could Prometheus base his great hope on the prospect that Zeus will be compelled to learn the

4. Kerényi, *Gods,* p. 101.

secret from him: from him whose mother had, as it were, saved him in advance by confiding in him her knowledge? This was the source of tension that entered into the drama the moment Prometheus announced to the chorus:

He, the lord of heaven, shall have need of me.

Prometheus and Io

O K E A N O S—he represents a lull in the rhythm of the tragedy—is permitted to hear no more than what has already come to his ears. Even his daughters, when left alone with Prometheus, obtain only the most general information (515–25):

CHORUS: *Who is the helmsman of necessity?*

PROMETHEUS: *Moira, threefold; Erinyes, unforgetting.*

CHORUS: *And Zeus is not so strong?*

PROMETHEUS: *He cannot shun what is foredoomed.*

CHORUS: *And he is not foredoomed to rule forever?*

PROMETHEUS: *No word of that. Ask me no further.*

CHORUS: *Some silent secret hides behind your silence.*

PROMETHEUS: *Think of another theme. It is not yet
the time to speak of this.
It must be wrapped in darkness, so alone*

> *I shall some time be saved*
> *from shame and grief and bondage.*

But after the song of the chorus Io appears, the unfortunate maiden condemned by Zeus to wander about the earth in the form of a heifer, and with her a climax ensues. A fantastic archaic world bursts into the drama, and with it a new suffering that demands consolation (752–74):

PROMETHEUS: *Hardly would you endure my trial,*
whose fate it is not ever to find death
that ends all pain. For me there is no end
until Zeus falls from power.

IO: *Zeus fall from power?*

PROMETHEUS: *You would rejoice, I think, to see that happen?*

IO: *How could I not, who suffer at his hands?*

PROMETHEUS: *Know then that it shall surely be.*

IO: *But who will strip the tyrant of his scepter?*

PROMETHEUS: *He will himself and his own empty mind.*

IO: *How? Tell me, if it is not wrong to ask.*

PROMETHEUS: *He will make a marriage that will vex him.*

IO: *Goddess or mortal, if it may be spoken?*

PROMETHEUS: *It may not be. Seek not to know.*

IO: *His wife will drive him from his throne?*

PROMETHEUS: *Her child shall be more than his father's match.*

IO: *And is there no way of escape for him?*

PROMETHEUS: *No way indeed, unless my bonds are loosed.*

IO: *But who can loose them against Zeus' will?*

PROMETHEUS: *A son of yours—so fate decrees.*

IO: *What words are these? A child of mine shall free you?*

PROMETHEUS: *Ten generations first must pass and then three more.*

What amazing prophecies are these! Words unique in pagan Greek literature, expressing something very close to the expectation of a savior. The second prophecy—concerning the descendant of Io in the thirteenth generation, who will unloose the Titan's bonds—aims clearly and distinctly at Herakles. After twelve generations, which could be named in accordance with a genealogical tradition, this son of Zeus will appear to free Prometheus. But he will be able to do so only if by then another son of Zeus, even greater than his father, has been born, who will overthrow and replace the ruler of the world. At the end of Zeus' work of world building it is also anticipated that he will marry, and with this marriage what he has founded will come to an end. An amazing possibility dawns: the possibility of a salvation from the intolerable oppression of the environing world, a transcending of the order of Zeus by something stronger which will grow from within it, for the order of Zeus encompasses all things that grow. In his thoughts Prometheus does not yet side with the new god, who will possibly be stronger than Zeus. The new god's victory would not be the solution which Prometheus hopes to obtain from Zeus, with Zeus, in this given world, but an incalculable dissolution of the existing order. If the king of the gods should plead with him, Prometheus might help him once more in the face of the new threat. And Herakles, the pre-destined deliverer, will come indeed, though not in opposition to the commandment of Zeus, as Io supposes. But Prometheus also considers the other possibility: that he may not help Zeus.

The Oracular Words of Prometheus

THUS, after the departure of Io, his prophecy becomes something other than a promise of liberation. It is a unique imaginative step beyond the world, beyond the cosmos, and shows the essentially limited character of the realm of Zeus. The existing cosmos means the encompassing and the encompassed, the chaining and the chained, Zeus and Prometheus, gods and men. Prometheus will not die but suffer—for thirty thousand years, an entire era. Saved from destruction (235), the human race will also endure. But something different from this world *might* happen. Prometheus rises above this world, as it were, not from pride and defiance but on the strength of a vision derived from a profound maternal source (908–27):

PROMETHEUS: *In very truth shall Zeus, for all his stubborn pride,*
be humbled, such a marriage he will make
to cast him down from throne and power.
And he shall be no more remembered.
The curse his father put on him
shall be fulfilled.
The curse that he cursed him with as he fell

from his age-long throne.
The way from such trouble no one of the gods
can show him save I.
These things I know and how they shall come to pass.
So let him sit enthroned in confidence,
trust to his crashing thunder high in air,
shake in his hands his fire-breathing dart.
Surely these shall be no defense,
but he will fall, in shame unbearable.
Even now he makes ready against himself
one who shall wrestle with him and prevail,
a wonder of wonders, who will find
a flame that is swifter than lightning,
a crash to silence the thunder,
who will break into pieces the sea-god's spear,
the bane of the ocean that shakes the earth.
Before this evil Zeus shall be bowed down.
He will learn how far apart are a king and a slave.

After these towering oracular words there is again a trough in the
waves of the tragedy: the arrival of Hermes with a threatening message from Zeus (947–48):

The great father gives you here his orders:
Reveal this marriage that you boast of,
by which he shall be hurled from power.

And then a last climax: the lightnings of Zeus fall upon Prometheus,
unyielding in the possession of his knowledge, invoking the eternal
witnesses. Hermes, too, has come to him with a knowledge. Not with
one befitting the son of Themis but with an account of the punishments—on the subject of which Prometheus believes himself to be
sufficiently well informed—that are still to come before something impossible, scarcely even conceivable, happens.

X. THE PROMETHEAN PROPHECY

The Foundation of the Prophecy

THE PROPHECIES of Prometheus seem to suggest the coming of a savior. We must pause for a moment to consider this more closely. Prometheus, it is true, does not set his hope in a salvation that would signify the end of the rule and order of Zeus. Thus it is not a redemption in the Buddhist or Gnostic-Christian sense of the word, but only a deliverance under the rule of Zeus and within his order. However, the idea of salvation in its absolute form, not yet molded by historical Christianity, seems to cut into the smooth, solid roundness of the Greek cosmos. Even though Prometheus expects only his liberation and not a salvation in the later Gnostic or Christian sense, still, the idea of the downfall of the just and unjust ruler of the cosmos makes its appearance in Aischylos. And so we pause to ask: Has this idea any foundation whatever in Greek mythology? Has it any foundation other than the story of how, when the present order was established, Father Kronos was overthrown by Zeus, his son? The strange part of it is that there actually is such a mythological foundation. Pindar speaks of it very simply, in a tone far removed from any eschatological implication, in his eighth Isthmian Ode (27–35).

Zeus and Poseidon vied for the glorious Thetis, a daughter of the ancient sea-god Nereus. Each desired the fair goddess for his wife. Eros had come over them. The gods, however, with their immortal designs did not permit the marriage to take place. For a prophecy had been imparted to them by Themis, the good counselor. It was decreed by Fate, she told them, that the sea-goddess should bear a son who would be mightier than his own father. Should he be begotten by Zeus or Poseidon, he would possess a mightier weapon than the thunderbolt or the trident. So runs Pindar's story in almost literal rendition. And the hopes of Aischylos' Prometheus accord with it. The source of his knowledge is the same goddess, Mother Themis. And he measures the power of the dreaded new god by the same standard (921–24):

> *a flame that is swifter than lightning,*
> *a crash to silence the thunder,*
> *who will break into pieces the sea-god's spear,*
> *the bane of the ocean that shakes the earth.*

Both poems, the Isthmian Ode and the Prometheus trilogy, stem from approximately the same period, the dawn of the classical century. Aischylos may have known Pindar's ode, in which the mention of the trident side by side with the thunderbolt is particularly justified by the context. We cannot know with certainty, but in any case this beautiful story of the marriage points back to a deeper and more solid foundation—more apt to sustain the structure of a cosmogonic drama—than any contemporary of Aischylos, even Pindar, could have invented. A free invention, springing from the mythological tradition but spun out by both poets before the eyes of all classical Greece, is also quite out of the question. A far more likely source of the tale would be the archaic epic poetry, communicating an older mythology than Homer, which in addition to the *Titanomachia* included a body of tales which precede the Iliad, the *Kypria,* so called because they are the work of a poet of Cyprus. In the *Kypria* Themis appears as the adviser of Zeus before the marriage of Thetis with the mortal Peleus [XV],[1] and this too may have been recounted in the sequel to that old story,

---

1. Kerényi, *Heroes,* pp. 308 f.

perhaps the *Titanomachia,* according to which the mother of Prometheus and the king of the gods formed an alliance.

The marriage of Thetis forms a turning point in the mythological history of the world in which the "cyclic" poetry of the Greeks—the great cycle of epics beginning with the *Kypria*—connected the world-founding deeds and victories of Zeus with the battles and sufferings of the heroes. These struggles and sufferings attained their summit, exemplary for the life of the archaic and classical Greeks, in Troy: and their most humanly moving and meaningful—in so far as meaning can illumine without consoling—climax in the fate of Achilles. At the divine pole reigns the indomitable victor, Zeus; at the human pole—in a very different way, for he is no sovereign—reigns the mortal-immortal son of Thetis, the fruit of her marriage with Peleus: Achilles.

The Son of Thetis

H Ö L D E R L I N does not depart too far from the Greek view of this Homeric figure when he tells us that he admires Homer most of all for his Achilles. "The love and intelligence with which he understood and sustained and elevated this character are unique," he once wrote.[2] "Take the aged lords Agamemnon and Ulysses and Nestor with their wisdom and their folly, take the blustering Diomedes, the blindly raging Ajax, and set them beside the inspired, all-powerful, melancholy, gentle son of the gods, Achilles, beside this *enfant gâté* of nature, and consider how the poet situated this youth, endowed with intelligence and

2. *Sämtliche Werke* (Hist.-krit. Ausgabe, ed. Hellingrath et al.), 247–48. To judge by their style, the sketches on Achilles are a part of the preparatory work for the *Hyperion*. To complement Hölderlin's picture of Achilles, cf. Kerényi, *Heroes,* pp. 347 ff.

grace and the strength of a lion, halfway between precocity and savagery, and you will find a miracle of art in the character of Achilles. The youth stands in striking contrast to Hektor, the noble, loyal, pious man whose heroism springs so completely from duty and a sensitive conscience, for Achilles owes everything to the richness and beauty of his nature. Yet, with all the contrast, there is a strong kinship between them, and this is what makes it so tragic when in the end Achilles appears as Hektor's mortal enemy. . . ."

Yet, over and above his conflict with Hektor, the essence of Achilles' tragic fate is that he "was so strong and vulnerable, the most successful and the most perishable flower of the heroic world," that he was so much a "creature of an hour," destined to an early death. "Just because he is so beautiful," Hölderlin adds, and this "just because" belongs only to him, not to an ancient author. The supreme human rank of Achilles is self-evident for Homer. The pre-eminence of Achilles in beauty was taken so much for granted that Homer alludes to it only in passing when he mentions the second most beautiful of the heroes.[3] It is more for this reason than because the goddess Eris had cast her famous apple, allotted to the fairest woman among the guests, that the marriage from which the most beautiful of heroes was to be born represents a turning point in the mythological history of the Greeks. It became the turning point which decided that the tragic would predominate in the most exemplary of human destinies, because it meant not only that the supreme flower of heroism, the most godlike of heroes, would be immersed in all the darkness of an archaic warrior's life but also that he would be the most mortal of all heroes.

The legend of how Achilles was carried off to a white isle of bliss, where he was made immortal, and Helen, the fairest of women, or

---

3. Iliad II 473.

Medeia, the moonlike granddaughter of Helios, was given him to wife, does not dispel the dark mist of earthly mortality, of voluntary death, which in the Iliad surrounds his head, glowing with noble anger. On the advice of Themis, Thetis was given in marriage to Peleus, a mortal hero, in order that she might bear *this* mortal son. But what a different turn in the history of the world, in the shaping of its order, this marriage might have meant, if Achilles had been born as the immortal son of Zeus or Poseidon! A tradition known to Pindar and Aischylos expresses this very thought in a prophecy of Themis.

The secret that raised Prometheus above the king of the gods consisted in the possibility of a salvation in the Greek style. Kindled for a brief moment by the image of Achilles, this idea gave it new beauty and lent new poignancy to the bitter fact that one so constituted should be so perishable. What might the world have been if he who was so beautiful, so strong, and so unlike all the despotic kings with their craving for power, so unlike Agamemnon, for instance; if this hero, who flared up in rage and softened in compassion—as indeed he softened toward Priam—had not been subject to death? if he had come to rule the world in Zeus' stead? In the tale of the preamble to the marriage of Peleus and Thetis, this impossible possibility cast a beam of light on the son of Thetis, the Expected One. For Prometheus he was the chief threat, though one never to be realized, to the power of Zeus.

With all this the Greek view of the world preserves its roundness. Yet now it is disclosed to us, not as an absolute but as merely the existing state of the world, which might just as well give place to another. And it is imperfect in another respect as well in relation to man and his needs. What, we may ask, is left for man? what salvation—what solution? Can a solution be gleaned from the remnants of the Aischylean trilogy?

XI. 'PROMETHEUS DELIVERED'

The Last Prophecy in the 'Prometheus Bound'

NOT WITHOUT preparation we approach the remnants of the *Prometheus Lyomenos*, the last drama of the trilogy. In this play, so the title tells us, Prometheus is set free. The question of whether he is merely released from his fetters or "saved"—though not in the absolute, Buddhist or Gnostic sense or even in the sense to which we have just alluded, which dawned for a moment on the Greek mind—may for the moment be left open. Prometheus himself has predicted that Herakles, a descendant of Io in the thirteenth generation, would set him free—after what torments and after the fulfillment of what unthinkable conditions, Hermes tells us at the end of the *Desmotes* (1020–29).

> *After long length of time you will return*
> *to see the light, but Zeus' winged hound,*
> *an eagle red with blood,*
> *shall come a guest unbidden to your banquet.*
> *All day long he will tear to rags your body,*
> *great rents within the flesh,*
> *feasting in fury on the blackened liver.*
> *Look for no ending to this agony*
> *until a god will freely suffer for you,*
> *will take on him your pain, and in your stead*
> *descend to where the sun is turned to darkness,*
> *the black depths of death.*

And immediately after this speech the first of Hermes' threats, that Zeus will hurl the Titan down to Tartaros with his lightnings, is carried out before our eyes. The rest is reserved for the third tragedy.

Bodily Pain

F I R S T, then, comes the new torment. While in *Prometheus Desmotes* we behold an image of injustice, here in the *Lyomenos* we see the torment of a constantly renewed wound: bodily pain. Cicero speaks of this kind of pain, *dolor*, as one—according to some philosophers, the greatest—of the evils of human existence, and cites, in Latin translation, the great speech of Prometheus from the third drama of Aischylos. In the second play it is the elements who witness the injustice suffered by Prometheus. In this third drama, the Titan chained to the Caucasus calls upon his delivered kinsmen to witness his torments.

> *Offspring of Titans, linked in blood to ours,*
> *Children of Heaven, see bound to rugged cliffs*
> *A prisoner, like a ship on roaring seas*
> *Which timid sailors anchor, fearing night.*
> *Jupiter, Saturn's son, thus nailed me here,*
> *Jove's power claimed the hands of Mulciber;* [1]
> *These wedges he by cruel art pinned in*
> *And burst my limbs, and by his skill, poor wretch,*
> *Pierced through, I make this Furies' fort my home.*
> *More, each third fatal day Jove's minister,*
> *In gloomy flight swoops here with talons bent,*
> *And tears me piecemeal for a savage feast.*
> *Then crammed with liver fat and gorged in full*
> *Pours forth an echoing scream and soaring up*
> *With feathered tail he strokes away my blood.*
> *When liver gnawn is swollen and grown afresh,*
> *Greedy he then comes back to hideous meal.*
> *Thus nourish I this guard of my sad torture*

---

1. Vulcanus, i.e., Hephaistos.

> *Which mars my living frame with endless woe.*
> *For, as ye see, bound in the chains of Jove*
> *I cannot keep that fell bird from my breast.*
> *Reft of myself I wait the torturing hour*
> *Looking for end of ill in hoping death.*[2]

A chorus of Titans is a rare occurrence on the Greek stage as we know it in the classical period; but it becomes conceivable when we consider that the tragic mask had originally been devised for ghostlike figures emerging from the underworld.[3] In the Heidelberg fragment, the Titans seem to have come from the underworld. Here, in the *Lyomenos,* the place and apparently the time are different.

> *But Zeus immortal set free the Titans,*

says Pindar in his fourth Pythian Ode (291), adding:

> *With time*
> *sails change as the winds die down.*[4]

The most likely explanation for the liberation of the Titans is that the thirty thousand years in which they were condemned to suffer have elapsed. Prometheus' term of punishment began later. Here again we must go back to events which were known to Aischylos from a mythological tradition most probably recorded in the *Titanomachia.* After Prometheus, the herald of the Titans, had helped Zeus to his victory, he no doubt celebrated his marriage to Hesione, a goddess and not merely a heroine as she was later held to be: it was then that there

---

2. Cicero, *Tusc.* II 10 (tr. King, pp. 171, 173). Also in Nauck, fr. 193 (and in Smyth, II, 448–50, fr. 107).

3. Kerényi, "Birth and Rebirth of Tragedy," *Diogenes,* no. 28 (Winter, 1959); *Streifzüge eines Hellenisten,* p. 45.

4. Tr. Lattimore, p. 69.

resounded the wedding song of the sea nymphs ("I stood beside your bridal bed, I sang the wedding hymn") which they recollect in the *Desmotes* (556). Then came the conflict and the first sacrifice at Mekone, then the theft of fire and punishment. During all this time the other Titans had been sitting in Erebos.

In trying to visualize the throng of Titans that now approaches, we should not suppose that Aischylos merely used masks for the names in the Hesiodic genealogy. It is scarcely conceivable and there is no tradition to the effect that the six Titanesses, well known as venerable great goddesses, were all present. The goddess Gē or Gaia, mother of the gods as well as the Titans and herself no Titaness, is mentioned side by side with Herakles and after Hermes in the cast of characters of the *Desmotes*, probably referring to the *Lyomenos*. It seems certain that her role in this tragedy was something more than to serve as leader of the chorus. Whichever of the once conquered and now reappearing primordial gods led the chorus, he did not merely announce that his ghostly relatives had come—"to behold," as we read in a quotation [5] —but joins them in a song describing the archaic mythological journey they have completed: "Leaving the Erythraean Sea's sacred stream, red of floor, and the mere by Okeanos, the mere of the Aethiopians that dazzles with its gleam of brass and that giveth nourishment unto all, where the all-seeing Sun doth ever, in warm outpourings of soft water, refresh his undying body and his wearied steeds." [6]

Departing from this ancient realm of the sun, the primordial gods, the oldest powers of the environing cosmos, have come to behold the

---

5. Nauck, fr. 190 (also available in Smyth, II, 447, fr. 104).
6. Nauck, fr. 192 (tr. Smyth, II, 447–48, fr. 105). Smyth's rendering has here been modified by the addition of a phrase from Jones's translation of Strabo's *Geography* (I 2 27; I, 23), where this fragment was recorded.

scene which dominates the third tragedy just as the image of injustice dominated the second. The sufferings of Prometheus have taken on a new intensity. In the second tragedy the injustice of human existence, embodied by a Titanic figure, represented the contrary pole to the happy life of the Olympian gods, represented by Hephaistos and Hermes. Here we behold a still more terrible aspect of human existence: man's suffering in his own flesh is displayed as a spectacle worthy to be seen and pitied even by primordial beings who themselves have suffered for thousands of years in Tartaros. Man's suffering forms a worthy counterpart even to their un-Olympian, elemental being. Now for the first time Prometheus clamors for death to put an end to his pain:

> *amore mortis terminum anquirens mali*
> (*yearning for death as end to misery*)

as Cicero writes,[7] unmistakably quoting Aischylos.

With this the tragic poet draws the ultimate conclusion from the mode of existence represented by Prometheus. Against injustice he is helped by the hope of immortality. As long as Prometheus identifies himself with the immortal gods, he is not fully immersed in the human mode of existence. But when in addition to injustice he is condemned to bear this other concomitant of human existence, bodily pain, his very immortality, his inability to die, becomes meaningless, and his mode of existence subjected to injustice and pain demands, in accordance with its own law, to be concluded by the one issue that is given to man, namely, death. The god, who represents the human counterpole to the divine pole of the Titans and Olympians, has fallen

----

7. *Tusc.* II 10 25.

to the bitterest fate of man, to *dolor* and *amor mortis*, pain and the longing for death. He abandons his last hope, which he had painted in such glowing colors. The prophecies lose their value if he would rather die at once than await their fulfillment.

Immortals Who Long to Die

I N this third tragedy, the hero, despite his divine nature, has fallen to terrifying depths. In view of his human plight, we can hardly help thinking, if not of a "salvation" of Prometheus, then of a "solution" offered him by the order of Zeus, putting an end as it were to a problematic situation. There is indeed a problematic situation. Whither has Prometheus been banished? To the outermost rim of the world of mortals. The situation is "geographical" only in so far as the place of torment is accessible to mortal men, although they could not bear so much pain (they would die), a situation not among the inhabitants of the earth, the primordial men or natural beings, but far away, at the "edge," so that it may be equated with the Caucasus.

However, there is no point in asking whether this Caucasus, where Prometheus now receives his kinsmen, is the same mountain crag where the daughters of Okeanos visited him. Because the place is at the edge, the Titans are able to come to him from the land of the sun, which extends from west to east by way of the south. Meanwhile Prometheus has also suffered below, in the underworld, whither Zeus had flung him at the end of the second tragedy. He is also listed among the penitents in Hades.[8] Above and below and then again

---

8. Horace, *Odes* II 13 37, 18 35, and *Epodes* 17 67.

above, at the edge. The place cannot be defined geographically, but it can mythologically and existentially as one resulting from the situation of a moonlike being who in his suffering hovers between full divinity and human vulnerability and suffering. From this place of suffering there are only two ways out: either to be a man and die, which in the order of Zeus is not granted to Prometheus the god, or to be a god, but then to abandon the painful human lot to which the Titan has condemned himself and to which now, in the Zeus world, he is confined.

The solution to the problem of Prometheus' liberation at the end of the tragedy becomes understandable on the basis of this situation. The strangeness of the solution recorded in the tradition is in keeping with this strange situation and so confirms it. Here any guesswork would be presumptuous. The last prediction of Hermes in the *Prometheus Bound* ended with the words (1026–29):

> Look for no ending to this agony
> until a god will freely suffer for you,
> will take on him your pain, and in your stead
> descend to where the sun is turned to darkness,
> the black depths of death.

One of the gods themselves—as Prometheus' substitute and heir to his torments—who, moreover, is prepared to enter into the darkness of Hades, the depths of Tartaros, in his place: this at first sight looks like the intentionally impossible condition on which the Titan may be released. But if we look more closely, we discern the tone of prophecy: the condition is meant seriously. To die and to suffer in Hades would not be impossible in the Zeus world. But what god would have taken this upon himself in order that Prometheus should replace him among the true immortals, the gods of the upper world, the earth, and the heavens, unless he felt that the descent to Hades would ease his own lot? Would his pain be appeased in the depths of the earth? These are questions which Aischylos surely did not ask of a tradition if he found one. But who was this god who *wished* to die? And who was it that *offered* his services to take the place of Prometheus? The god who wished to die or someone else?

In *Prometheus Lyomenos,* the offerer must have been Herakles. Like Io in the *Desmotes,* now in the *Lyomenos* the son of Zeus appears on his journey in search of the apples of the Hesperides. The Garden of the Hesperides lay at the edge, beyond the back of Atlas, regardless of whether he bore the axis of the sky in the west or in the north. Like the throng of Titans coming from the south, Herakles, perhaps after killing Emathion, a son of Eos and Tithonos, the gods of the morning, comes to the edge of the world where Prometheus is suffering.[9] He comes on a day when Prometheus is expecting the eagle. According to Aischylos, who deviates from Hesiod in this point, the terrible bird came not daily but only every second day. (Only! In order that Prometheus should be cheated of his hope, the hope of one plagued by recurrent tortures, that perhaps this time he will not come.) It is early morning, and the hero stands before him. Was it at this moment or later that he cried out: "Of his sire, mine enemy, this dearest son"?[10]

This line tells us but one thing, that the sufferer's spirit has not yet been broken by pain. He has learned to love death but not to love Zeus. We also have some quotations from a speech of Prometheus

9. Kerényi, *Heroes,* p. 173.
10. Nauck, fr. 201 (also in Smyth, II, 453, fr. 114).
ἐχθροῦ πατρός μοι τοῦτο φίλτατον τέκνον.

telling Herakles the way to the Garden of the Hesperides.[11] Then the eagle approaches. The hunter of all death-dealing monsters awakens in the son of Zeus. He sees the traces of blood on the tail of the giant bird. What has he learned from Prometheus? What need he have learned? To Apollo the Hunter, he cries: "May hunter Apollo speed my arrow straight!"[12] [IV, V]

And so the eagle is slain. But is Prometheus set free? Was Herakles permitted to remove his chains? Who may have prevented him? his father's thunder? Did the earth tremble and did Gē appear to sustain the order of the now firmly established Zeus world? Did she tell both of them that the liberation was impossible? that Prometheus with his torments must sink once more into the depths unless a god changed places with him? In the mythographic tradition, in a compendium of the myths of gods and heroes, bearing the name of the learned Apollodoros,[13] it is twice related that Herakles had offered Zeus Chiron the centaur, a god who wished to die, in exchange for Prometheus.[14] The story has also come down to us that when Herakles fought the centaurs in the Pholoe mountains one of his arrows, intended for another centaur, passed through its target and struck Chiron in the knee. Though Herakles loved and honored Chiron, he could not heal him, for these arrows were poisonous, having been dipped in the blood of the Hydra. The wounded Chiron, an immortal son of Kronos, withdrew to his cave with his incurable pain and there, like

11. Nauck, fr. 195–99 (also in Smyth, II, 451 ff., fr. 109–12, which, however, lacks Nauck, fr. 197).

12. Nauck, fr. 200 (tr. Smyth, II, 453, fr. 113, modified).

Ἀγρεὺς δ᾽ Ἀπόλλων ὀρθὸν ἰθύνοι βέλος.

13. *Library* II 5 11 and 4 (tr. Frazer, I, 230–31 and 228–29, respectively).

14. In the one passage (II 5 11), there is no doubt that the subject of the sentence παρέσχε τῶι Διὶ Χείρωνα θνήσκειν ἀθάνατον ἀντ᾽ αὐτοῦ θέλοντα is Herakles; in the other (II 5 4) this name, required by the sense, must be supplied. This was done by Kraus, col. 679.

Prometheus waiting in the Caucasus, awaited his redemption.

According to the *Titanomachia*,[15] it was Chiron who had set the human race on the path of justice by teaching men the oath and the sacrifice and the signs of heaven. This no doubt is why in the Iliad (XI 832) he is called the most righteous among the centaurs. Even if the idea of Chiron taking the place of Prometheus did not originate with Aischylos—a possibility that cannot be wholly excluded—the theme takes on a special significance in this play. The whole situation —the coming of one who will take Prometheus' sufferings upon himself—*compels* us to speak of a "redemption." Not only because Chiron buys the freedom of Prometheus with his own but because the possibility of a substitution proves that this is an existential suffering, not identified with any one person but inherent in existence. Whether borne by Prometheus or by another, the suffering goes on, and still there is no gap in the ranks of the gods. Where a man or god is saved from such depths, we may speak of "redemption."

The Redemption

THE situation is wonderfully pregnant. What contradictions and complementaries converge in this redemption of Prometheus! Herakles, the deliverer, could not relieve Prometheus of his pain. But he could, by mistake, cause incurable suffering in Chiron, whom he loved and honored. And Chiron, the primordial physician, who had taught renowned heroes so many things including medicine, knew his poisoned wound would never heal. This centaur, who as the son of

---

15. In Kinkel, *Epicorum graecorum fragmenta*, fr. 6, pp. 6–8.
εἴς τε δικαιοσύνην γένος ἤγαγε δείξας
ὅρκους καὶ θυσίας ἱερὰς καὶ σχήματ' Ὀλύμπου.

Kronos was almost equal in birth to Zeus, was the savior, prepared to vanish in Hades instead of Prometheus, taking with him the pain inflicted by Herakles. A healer, he crept away with his pain into the darkness of his cave like a sick animal, and longed to die. These contradictions and complementaries were inherent in the being of Chiron: it was his very nature to be a healer afflicted with pain, an immortal who suffered for others. Strange guarantor and eternal witness of this painful aspect of our existence, he became the redeemer of Prometheus.

So far, we have followed the tradition only to the point where Herakles offers Zeus Chiron in exchange for Prometheus. Before Zeus can consent, something else must come to pass—and this too is predicted in the *Prometheus Bound.* A condition remains to be fulfilled. The Titan has spoken of it in a tone very different from that of his other prophecies. The daughters of Okeanos, impressed by the amazing inventions of Prometheus, by all he had done to alleviate the life of man, already looked upon him as a god, not inferior to Zeus (508–10):

> *I have good hope that one day, loosed from your bonds,*
> *you shall be strong as Zeus.*

But Prometheus replies soberly (511–13):

> *Not thus—not yet—is fate's appointed end,*
> *fate that brings all to pass.*
> *I must be bowed by age-long pain and grief.*
> *So only will my bonds be loosed.*

Here the crucial word is "bowed." When Prometheus welcomes Herakles as the son of a detested father, he is not yet bowed. His

hatred of Zeus is no doubt dispelled when the whole world order op-
poses his liberation and he is compelled to recognize that his suffering is eternal, though perhaps it will be transferred to someone else. Is
it the goddess Gē, Mother Earth, who tells him this? Here we have a
lacuna that cannot be filled in. All we can safely say is that the Titan,
now "bowed," reveals to Zeus his secret knowledge—or rather, that of
his mother Themis—about the possible successor to the throne of the
gods.

Apart from the preparation for it in the *Desmotes*, this development
is supported by two testimonies. The one is to be found in the Late
Roman commentaries on Virgil's sixth Eclogue. The poem [16] mentions the "birds of Caucasus" and the "theft of Prometheus" (42).
In this connection one commentator relates at some length and another more briefly [17] what would seem to be the content of the *Prometheus Delivered*, namely, that Herakles, after slaying the eagle, still
feared to offend his father by delivering Prometheus. Thereupon Prometheus turned to Zeus, warning him not to marry Thetis, for the son
he would beget by her would overthrow him. In gratitude for the
warning, Zeus released the Titan from his chains but, in reminder of
his captivity, gave him a wreath and a ring to bear. This is how Prometheus was redeemed in an order which is characterized in the
second tragedy by the words (50): "No one is free but Zeus." [18]

An earlier and more authoritative witness is Catullus, but even his
testimony does not definitely prove that all the particulars mentioned
by the Virgil commentators stem from Aischylos. Catullus was prob-

---

16. Tr. Fairclough, I, 45.
17. The longer account is that of Probus (ed. Thilo and Hagen, III, fasc. 2, 344–
45), the shorter is by Servius (ibid., III, fasc. 1, 72).
18. ἐλεύθερος γὰρ οὔτις ἐστὶ πλὴν Διός.

ably drawing on an Alexandrian poem when among the divine guests at the wedding of Peleus and Thetis he included Prometheus

> *Extenuata gerens veteris vestigia poenae*
> *(Bearing the faded scars of the ancient penalty)*:[19]

that is, the ring. After all, was not this marriage, which replaced that of Zeus and Thetis, *his* doing? Thus his presence here, in the company of Zeus, his spouse, and his children, can only be taken as an allusion to the services he had rendered in the famous scene of the tragedy. For, according to the epic tradition reflected in the *Kypria*, Themis herself was the counselor who should have appeared. But does the ring, which recalls the past sufferings of the counselor, also stem from the *Prometheus Lyomenos*?

The ring cannot be definitely assigned to the final scene of the *Prometheus Delivered*. Aischylos may—this too is not excluded—have taken it from the cult of the Kabeiroi on Samothrace. On Samothrace, an island near Lemnos, iron rings were regarded, down to late antiquity, as mementos of a mystical bond between the mysterious great gods and those initiated into the mysteries of the Kabeiroi. Texts relating to the wearing of rings in antiquity [20] make it clear that iron rings were a sign of membership in the Samothracian cult, and this became all the more certain when a ring of this kind was found at the site of the Kabeirian sanctuary itself.[21] If Aischylos or another poet had the Titan appear with this emblem after his reconciliation with Zeus, he cannot have done so without some foundation in the traditions concerning both Prometheus and the Kabeiroi. This foundation—this ele-

19. LXIV 295 (tr. Cornish, p. 119).
20. Welcker, *Die Aeschylische Trilogie*, p. 52.
21. Kerényi, *Unwillkürliche Kunstreisen*, p. 102.

ment common to both mythical spheres, which could be transferred from one to the other—was no doubt the idea that the giving of the ring meant the forgiveness of Titanic sins. The rites of initiation into the mysteries of Samothrace included a confession of sins.[22]

The two possibilities—that Aischylos introduced the ring conferred at the end of the trilogy or that a Hellenistic poet first connected the ring with the wreath as a second symbol of forgiveness and reconciliation—stand side by side. To decide in favor of Aischylos would require us to venture too far into the realm of the unknowable in reconstructing the scene. Another character would have to enter to confer the ring or, supposing that the ring might be taken from Prometheus' chains, to bring a message about the ring from Zeus. Two pictures on Etruscan mirrors [XII–XIII], which in general reflect the state of Greek mythology shortly after 400 B.C., actually do show two helpers at the liberation of Prometheus. In the first, Herakles and Apollo stand on either side of the chained Prometheus, and this is in keeping with the invocation of Apollo Agreus in Aischylos. In the other, the two persons would seem to be the Dioskuroi, Kastor and Polydeukes—suggested also by the two stars above the Titan's head—each holding a ring. The inscriptions, the eagle on the ground, and the attributes of Herakles tell us, however, that Herakles, under the name of Calanice [Kallinikos] had taken Polydeukes' place. The ring in his hand is not meaningless, since he too was in need of forgiveness for slaying the eagle, but the conveyor of the ring is Kastor. He and his twin brother, who is here replaced by another son of Zeus, the slayer of the eagle, constituted a pair of Kabeiroi on Samothrace. We learn that both or one of them brought the ring, but whether this occurred in Aischylos is not certain.

22. Kerényi, "The Mysteries of the Kabeiroi," p. 45.

It is a different matter with the wreath. Aischylos relates—the passage has come down to us [23]—that men began to wear wreaths in honor of Prometheus and in exchange for his fetters. Thus the wearing of wreaths would seem to mean: to bear human existence in the Greek way. And there was no need to bring in a wreath for Prometheus. What distinguished wreaths from the pliable fronds that grew everywhere was their form: the bending. In Greek this is called *koróne*, while the original meaning of the Latin *corona*, borrowed from the Greek, is "wreath." On vase paintings from the Kabeirian sanctuary of Thebes, the grotesque beings who represent the Kabeiroi or first men on their way to the festival or rite [24] wear fronds instead of wreaths in their hair: wreaths seem to point to consummation of the rite. After "bowing," as he himself had predicted in the second tragedy, Prometheus "bent" the first wreath: the Greek word for both is *kámptein*. He

> *must be bowed by age-long pain and grief.*

Afterwards he bent the wreath.

In the passage cited (see p. 120), where Herakles offered Zeus Chiron in Prometheus' stead, we read that he took an olive branch "as a fetter" for himself, for he too, after his act of violence against the order of Zeus, was in need of atonement, which was expressed in the form and in the wearing of the wreath. In Attica, a land of olive trees, it was only natural to wear olive wreaths in memory of the beneficent Titan. In other sources, the wreath of Prometheus is described as consisting of the willowlike boughs of the *lygos* or *agnos*, the chaste tree (*Vitex agnus-castus*). In summer, when it blooms, this beautiful

23. Nauck, fr. 235 (also in Smyth, II, 460 f., fr. 128).
24. Wolters-Bruns, *Das Kabirenheiligtum von Theben*, I, pl. 33.

plant dominates the landscape of both Samothrace and Hera's island of Samos.

The learned Athenaios,[25] citing the Samian author Menodotos (672 f), tells us that the original inhabitants of these islands, the Carians, wore *lygos* wreaths. An age-old *lygos* tree on Samos was sacred to Hera herself; according to the Samian tradition, she was born under it. Assuredly the *lygos* tree was related to the great goddess, perhaps as a queen reigning in all her glory, but more likely to another aspect. At the time of her disappearing, at the darkest phase of her moonlike existence, the cult image of Hera was hidden in a *lygos* thicket.[26] The *lygos* wreath, borne in voluntary submission as in a rite, was befitting also to the nature of Prometheus as we have seen it: a moonlike being comparable to human existence darkened by suffering. The wreath of Prometheus delivered, an olive or a *lygos* frond bent to encircle the head, this sign and token of release and redemption, of repentance and reconciliation with Zeus, was the symbol of a bond with the hard laws of a luminous, rigidly established heaven consciously accepted by an eternally restless being, a victim of injustice, a sufferer from his own darkness, exposed to unendurable torments.

But Prometheus' wound was not forgotten. Of course it might have healed of itself, like the wounds of the gods. Or was it Chiron who appeared on the stage, healed the Titan, and then, driven by his own pain, rushed off to the underworld? We shall never know. But in a later representation of the scene, which, however, cannot have been more recent than the third century B.C., Chiron is replaced by the god who by then had taken over the role of the healing centaur in the entire Greek world and in Italy. On a third-century Etruscan mirror

25. *The Deipnosophists* (cf. LCL edn., VII, 102–3).
26. Kerényi, *Saeculum*, I (1950), p. 245.

found in a tomb near Bolsena, there is a scene that moves us strangely [XIV]. It recalls a Descent from the Cross. After the manner of the Etruscan art of the period the solemnity of the scene is emphasized by a temple in the background. Before the temple we see Prometheus in an attitude suggesting that he had just been taken down from his cliff. He is leaning on a god and a goddess, while Herakles merely sits resting. The names of the deities are inscribed in their Etruscan forms: the goddess is Athene, the god is Asklepios the healer, in the form of a handsome youth. We spoke at the beginning of the present work of "a striking resemblance and a striking contrast" between Prometheus and the Christian Saviour. The Titan was no redeemer, but was himself in need of redemption. Nor was he revered by the Greeks as a savior, a *sōtér*. But Asklepios was. The Greeks called him Sōtér, and for Prometheus—as for all mankind—he *was* the Savior.[27]

27. This representation is at the same time an extension of my book *Asklepios*. Another postscript to *Asklepios* might be provided by a reading in the Paian of Isyllos of Epidauros which I recommended but which was inadvertently omitted on p. 115, n. 12. Read as follows:

ἐκ δέ Φλεγύα γένετο, Αἴγλα δ' ὀνομάσθη·
τόδ' ἐπώνυμον· τόκ' ἄλλως δὲ Κορωνὶς ἐπεκλήθη—

and not

ἐκ δὲ Φλεγύα γένετο, Αἴγλα δ' ὀνομάσθη.
τόδ' ἐπώνυμον· τὸ κάλλος δὲ Κορωνὶς ἐπεκλήθη.

XII. CONCLUSION AFTER GOETHE

THE WORDS with which Aischylos expressed the final release in *Prometheus Delivered* have not been preserved. Goethe's words about the "Limits of Humanity"—those limits which for the Greeks expressed themselves in the unyielding cosmos and at the same time in the figures of the eternal gods—are no doubt softer and more effusive than any lines spoken by Aischylos. Yet, in the insight and attitude they express, they come closer than anything else that has ever been written to the meaning of Prometheus and his Greek redemption:

Limits of Humanity

When the primeval
Heavenly Father,
With hand indifferent
Out of dark-rolling clouds
Scatters hot lightnings
Over the earth,
Kiss I the lowest
Hem of His garment,
Kneeling before Him
In child-like trust.

For with the gods may
No mortal himself
At any time measure.
Should he be lifted
Up, till he touches
The stars with his forehead,

Nowhere to rest finds
The insecure feet,
And he is plaything
Of clouds and of winds.

Stands he with strong-knit
Marrowy bone
On the deep-seated
Enduring Earth,
No farther he reaches
Than but with the oak
Or the slenderer vine
Himself to compare.

What doth distinguish
Immortals from mortals?
In that many billows
Before those roll ever,
A stream flowing by:
Upheaveth a billow,
Collapses a billow,
And we are no more.

A little ring
Encloses our life,
And numerous races
Are strung through the cycles
On to existence's
Infinite chain.[1]

1. From *Poems of Goethe;* tr. Gibson, pp. 311–12.

PLATES

*Prometheus and Minerva (Pallas Athene), and (right) the workshop of Vulcan
(Hephaistos). Engraving from Montfaucon,* L'Antiquité expliquée et representée
en figures *(1719), a source for Hederich and Goethe. Cf. p. 17. The engraving reverses
the order of the figures from left to right (see* IIa *and* III*)*

a Prometheus sarcophagus, the original of the left two-thirds of the Montfaucon engraving (I). First half of the III century B. C. *Rome, Capitoline Museum. For scenes on the ends, see III and IV. Fully described in Robert,* Die antiken Sarkophagreliefs, *III, pt. 3, no. 355*

b Another Prometheus sarcophagus. Right of center, the theft of fire—here carried in a torch-holder, not a fennel-stalk—from the workshop of Hephaistos. Cf. p. 80. Middle of the II century B. C. *Paris, Louvre. Fully described in Robert, no. 351*

Workshop of Hephaistos. In the left background, the men without fire. Cf. p. 80.
Leftward end of the Prometheus sarcophagus in the Capitoline Museum (IIa), original
of the right third of the Montfaucon engraving (I)

Liberation of Prometheus. Cf. pp. 40, 120. Rightward end of the Prometheus sarcophagus in the Capitoline Museum (IIa)

IV

Liberation of Prometheus. Cf. pp. 38, 40, 120. Crater, VI *century* B. C. *Berlin, Staatliche Museen*

Prometheus and Atlas. Cf. p. 38. Laconian cylix, VI *century* B. C. *Rome, Gregorian Etruscan Museum*

Hera and Prometheus. Cf. p. 59. Cylix, v century B. C. *Paris, Bibliothèque Nationale*

Prometheus among the satyrs (lower band). Cf. pp. 66, 69. Calyx crater, v *century* B. C. *Oxford, Ashmolean Museum*

Prometheus among the satyrs. Cf. pp. 66, 69. Detail from the Oxford calyx crater (VIII)

a   *Prometheus among the satyrs. Cf. pp. 66, 69. Scene from the Feuardent calyx crater. From Tischbein,* Hamilton Vases

b   *Original men before the deities "Pais" and "Kabiros." Cf. pp. 61, 69. Shards,* IV *century* B. C., *from the Kabeirion at Thebes. Athens, National Museum*

Prometheus among the satyrs. Cf. pp. 69, 70. Detail from a lekane lid, v century B. C.
Berlin, Staatliche Museen

Prometheus between Herakles and Apollo. Cf. p. 125. Etruscan mirror. From Gerhard, Etruskische Spiegel

*Prometheus between Herakles and Kastor. Cf. p. 125. Etruscan
mirror, IV or III century B.C. From Gerhard,* Etruskische Spiegel

Prometheus with Asklepios, Athene, and Herakles. Cf.
p. 128. Etruscan mirror, III century B.C. New York,
Metropolitan Museum of Art

Thetis between the Nereids and Peleus (upper band). Cf. p. 108. Plaque from a bronze tripod, VII century B.C. New York, Metropolitan Museum of Art

Primitive smelting furnace. Matakam tribe, northern Cameroons. Cf. p. 70.
The branches are probably for protection against the "vapors"

LIST OF WORKS CITED

These are used in the notes and in the List of Works Cited. Shortened titles readily identified in the List of Works Cited are not included.

AJA   *American Journal of Archaeology.* Princeton, N. J.

Arch RW   *Archiv für Religionswissenschaft.* Freiburg im Breisgau.

EJ   *Eranos Jahrbuch.* Zurich.

FGrHist   FELIX JACOBY. *Die Fragmente der griechischen Historiker.* Berlin and Leiden, 1923–59. 3 vols. in 11 parts.

LCL   Loeb Classical Library. London and Cambridge, Mass. (earlier, New York).

OCT   Oxford Classical Texts (Scriptorum Bibliotheca Oxoniensis).

RE   AUGUST PAULY and GEORG WISSOWA (eds.). *Real-Encyclopädie der classischen Altertumswissenschaft.* Stuttgart, 1894 ff.

In general, classical texts are unlisted except when an edition or translation has been cited.

AESCHYLUS (AISCHYLOS). Fragments. In: *Tragicorum graecorum fragmenta*. Edited by August Nauck. Leipzig, 1861.

———. ———. In: [*Works*]. With an English translation by Herbert Weir Smyth. (LCL.) 1922–26. 2 vols. (II.)

———. ———. Other Aischylos fragments are included in the works of CICERO, LOBEL, and SIEGMANN, respectively (q.v.).

———. *Prometheus Bound (Prometheus Desmotes)*. In: *Aeschyli septem quae supersunt tragoediae*. Edited by Gilbert Murray. (OCT.) Oxford, 1937.

———. ———. In: *Aeschylus: Prometheus and Other Plays*. Translated, with an introduction, by Philip Vellacott. (Penguin Classics.) Harmondsworth and Baltimore, 1961.

———. ———. In: *Three Greek Plays: Prometheus Bound, Agamemnon, The Trojan Women*. Translated, with an introduction, by Edith Hamilton. New York, [1937].

———. Scholia on *Prometheus*. In: THOMAS STANLEY (ed.). *Aeschyli tragoediae septem cum scholiis graecis omnibus*. London, 1663.

———. *The Suppliant Maidens*. In: [*Works*]. For other details see above under Fragments. (I.)

ALCMAN. Fragments. In: *Lyra graeca*. Edited and translated by J. M. Edmonds. (LCL.) 1922–27. 3 vols. (I.)

APOLLODORUS. *The Library*. With an English translation by Sir James George Frazer. (LCL.) 1912–21. 2 vols. (I.)

APOLLONIUS RHODIUS. *Argonautica*. With an English translation by R. C. Seaton. (LCL.) 1912.

———. *Scholia in Apollonium Rhodium vetera*. Edited by Karl Wendel. (Bibliothecae graecae et latinae auctarium Weidmannianum, IV.) Berlin, 1935.

[ARATUS.] See THEON.

ATHENAEUS. *The Deipnosophists.* With an English translation by Charles Burton Gulick. (LCL.) 1927–41. 7 vols. (IV, VII.)

BEAZLEY, J. D. "Prometheus Fire-Lighter." *AJA*, XLIII (1939).

BLIXEN, KAREN, Baroness; pseud. ISAK DINESEN. *Out of Africa.* New York, 1938; London, 1937. (Reprinted in: The Modern Library, New York, 1952; Penguin Books, Harmondsworth, 1954.)

BOLL, FRANZ. "Kronos-Helios." *Arch RW*, XIX (1916–19).

BROWNING, ELIZABETH BARRETT. "Prometheus Bound." In: *Poetical Works.* London, 1897.

CATULLUS, GAIUS VALERIUS. Poems. Translated by Francis Warre Cornish. In: *Catullus, Tibullus, and Pervigilium Veneris.* (LCL.) 1913.

CENSORINUS. *De die natali liber.* Edited by Friedrich Hultsch. (Bibliotheca Teubneriana.) Leipzig, 1867.

Century Dictionary. New York, 1900–1902. 10 vols. (II.)

CICERO, MARCUS TULLIUS. *Tusculan Disputations.* With an English translation by J. E. King. (LCL.) 1927.

DIELS, HERMANN (ed.). *Die Fragmente der Vorsokratiker.* 6th edn., Berlin, 1951–52. 3 vols. (For a partial English translation of the fifth edition, see FREEMAN.)

DINESEN, ISAK. See BLIXEN, KAREN.

DÖRIG, J., and OLOF GIGON. *Der Kampf der Götter und Titanen.* Olten and Lausanne, 1961.

ECKHART, LOTHAR. "Prometheus in der bildenden Kunst." In: *RE*, ser. 2, XLV, s.v. "Prometheus," cols. 702–30.

EITREM, SAMSON. "De Prometheo." *Eranos* (Göteborg), XLIV (1946).

EMPEDOKLES. In: DIELS (q.v.).

EUPHORION. Scholia. In: JOHN UNDERSHELL POWELL (ed.). *Collectanea Alexandrina: reliquiae minores poetarum graecorum aetatis Ptolemaicae 323–146 A.C., epicorum, elegiacorum, lyricorum, ethicorum.* Oxford, 1925.

EURIPIDES. *Ion.* In: [*Plays*]. With an English translation by Arthur S. Way. (LCL.) 1912. 4 vols. (IV.)

———. *The Phoenician Maidens.* Ibid. (III.)

FRAZER, Sir JAMES GEORGE. See APOLLODORUS.

FREEMAN, KATHLEEN (tr.). *Ancilla to the Pre-Socratic Philosophers.* Cambridge, Mass., 1948. (A complete translation of the Fragments in DIELS, fifth edition, without the commentary.)

GARDI, RENÉ. *Der schwarze Hephaestus.* Bern, 1954.

GERHARD, EDUARD. *Etruskische Spiegel (Miroirs étrusques).* Berlin, 1841–97. 5 vols. (II, nos. 138, 139.)

GOETHE, JOHANN WOLFGANG VON. *Dichtung und Wahrheit.* In: *Werke* (Gedenk-ausgabe). Edited by Ernst Beutler. Zurich, 1948–54. 24 vols. (X.) (For an English translation of *Dichtung und Wahrheit* see *Poetry and Truth from My Own Life,* below.)

――――. Letters. Ibid. (XVIII, XXI.)

――――. "Limits of Humanity." In: *Poems of Goethe.* Translated by William Gibson. London, 1883.

――――. *Pandora* [play]. In: *Werke* (see above). (VI, 406–43.)

――――. *Poetry and Truth from My Own Life.* Translated by Minna Steele Smith. London, 1908. 2 vols. (II.)

――――. *Prometheus* [dramatic fragment]. In: *Werke* (see above). (IV, 185–97, and notes, 1037–40.)

――――. "Prometheus" [monologue]. Ibid. (I, 320 f.)

GREY, Sir GEORGE. *Polynesian Mythology: An Ancient Traditional History of the New Zealand Race, as Furnished by Their Priests and Chiefs.* London, 1855. (Reprinted by Whitcombe and Tombs Ltd., London, 1929.)

HECATAEUS (HEKATAIOS). Fragments. See JACOBY.

HEDERICH, BENJAMIN. *Reales Schullexicon.* Leipzig, 1731.

Hesiod, the Homeric Hymns, and Homerica. With an English translation by Hugh G. Evelyn-White. (LCL.) 1920.

HESIOD. Fragments. In: *Hesiodi Carmina.* Edited by Aloisius Rzach. (Bibliotheca scriptorum graecorum et romanorum Teubneriana.) 3rd edn., Leipzig, 1913.

――――. *Theogony.* In: *Hesiod . . .* (q.v.).

――――. *Works and Days.* Ibid.

HESIOD. Scholia on HESIOD'S *Erga kai Hemerai* [*Works and Days*]. *See* PROKLOS DIADOCHOS.

HESYCHIOS OF ALEXANDRIA. *Hesychii Alexandrini lexicon post Ioannem Albertum.* Edited by Maurice Schmidt. Jena, 1858–62. 4 vols. (II.)

HIPPOLYTUS. *Refutatio omnium haeresium* [*Philosophumena*, or *Elenchos*]. In: *Philosophumena; or, The Refutation of All Heresies.* Translated by Francis Legge. London, 1921. 2 vols. (I.)

HÖLDERLIN, FRIEDRICH. *Sämtliche Werke.* Edited by Norbert von Hellingrath, Friedrich Seebass, and Ludwig von Pigenot. (Historisch-kritische Ausgabe.) Berlin, 1943. 4 vols. (III.)

HOMER. *The Iliad.* Translated by E. V. Rieu. (Penguin Classics.) Harmondsworth and Baltimore, 1960.

Homeric Hymns. In: *Homeri opera.* Edited by Thomas W. Allen. 2nd edn., Oxford, 1908–12. 5 vols. (V.)

HYGINUS. *Astronomica.* Edited by Bernhard Bunte. Leipzig, 1875.

———. *Fabulae.* Edited by Moritz Schmidt. Jena, 1872.

Inscriptiones graecae. Consilio et auctoritate Academiae Litterarum Regiae Borussicae editum. 2nd edn., Berlin, 1873 ff. 14 vols. (XII.)

JACOBY, FELIX. *FGrHist.* (Duris of Samos in II; Hekataios in I.)

KERÉNYI, C. [in some publications KARL]. *Die antike Religion.* 3rd edn., Düsseldorf, 1952. (For an English translation see *The Religion of the Greeks and Romans,* below.)

———. *Apollon: Studien über antike Religion und Humanität.* 3rd edn., Düsseldorf, 1953.

———. *Asklepios: Archetypal Image of the Physician's Existence.* Translated by Ralph Manheim. (Archetypal Images in Greek Religion, 3.) New York (Bollingen Series LXV) and London, 1959. (Original: *Der göttliche Arzt: Studien über Asklepios und seine Kultstätten.* 2nd edn., Darmstadt, 1956.)

———. "Birth and Rebirth of Tragedy: From the Origin of Italian Opera to the Origin of Greek Tragedy." *Diogenes* (Chicago, Ill.), no. 28, Winter, 1959. (Original: *Streifzüge eines Hellenisten,* pp. 29 ff., q.v.)

———. "Dionysos und unsere Religionsgeschichte." *Wiener humanistische Blätter,* 1958, pp. 24–25.

―――. *Der frühe Dionysos*. Oslo, 1961.

―――. *Die Geburt der Helena*. (Albae Vigiliae, N.S. 3.) Zurich, 1945. (The chapter "Mysterien der Kabiren" was first published in *EJ 1944*, XI [1945], 11–60; for an English version see "The Mysteries of the Kabeiroi.")

―――. *Geistiger Weg Europas: Fünf Vorträge über Freud, Jung, Heidegger, Thomas Mann, Hofmannsthal, Rilke, Homer, und Hölderlin*. (Albae Vigiliae, N.S. 16.) Zurich, 1955.

―――. *The Gods of the Greeks*. Translated by Norman Cameron. London and New York, 1951. (Reprinted with different pagination in Pelican Books, Harmondsworth, 1958.)

―――. *Griechische Miniaturen*. Zurich, 1957.

―――. *Hermes der Seelenführer: Das Mythologem vom männlichen Lebensursprung*. (Albae Vigiliae, N.S. 1.) Zurich, 1944.

―――. *The Heroes of the Greeks*. Translated by H. J. Rose. London, 1959.

―――. *Die Jungfrau und Mutter der griechischen Religion: Eine Studie über Pallas Athene*. (Albae Vigiliae, N.S. 12.) Zurich, 1952.

―――. *Die Mysterien von Eleusis*. Zurich, 1962.

―――. "The Mysteries of the Kabeiroi." In: *The Mysteries*, q.v. (For German versions, see *Die Geburt der Helena*.)

―――. "Mythologie und Gnosis." *EJ 1940/41*, VIII (1942).

―――. *Mythologie und Gnosis*. (Albae Vigiliae, 14.) n.p., 1942.

―――. *Niobe: Neue Studien über antike Religion und Humanität*. Zurich, 1949.

―――. "The Primordial Child in Primordial Times." In: CARL GUSTAV JUNG and C. KERÉNYI. *Essays on a Science of Mythology: The Myth of the Divine Child and the Mysteries of Eleusis*. Translated by R. F. C. Hull. (Bollingen Series XXII.) New York, 1950. (London, 1951; titled *Introduction to a Science of Mythology*.) (Original: *Einführung in das Wesen der Mythologie*. Amsterdam and Leipzig, 1941; new edn., Zurich, 1951.)

―――. *The Religion of the Greeks and Romans*. London, 1962. (Revised edition and translation of *Die antike Religion*, q.v.)

―――. *Streifzüge eines Hellenisten*. Zurich, 1960.

―――. *Tochter der Sonne*. Zurich, 1944.

KERÉNYI, C. "The Trickster in Relation to Greek Mythology." In: PAUL RADIN. *The Trickster: A Study in American Indian Mythology*. With commentaries by Karl Kerényi and C. G. Jung. London, 1956. (Original: *Der göttliche Schelm*. Zurich, 1954.)

————. *Umgang mit Göttlichem*. Göttingen, 1955.

————. *Unwillkürliche Kunstreisen: Fahrten im alten Europa, 1952–53*. (Albae Vigiliae, N.S. 13–14.) Zurich, 1954.

————. "Zeus und Hera: Der Kern der olympischen Götterfamilie." *Saeculum* (Munich), I (1950).

KRAUS, WALTHER. "Prometheus." In: *RE*, ser. 2, XLV.

KRETSCHMER, PAUL. "Die protindogermanische Schicht." *Glotta* (Göttingen), XIV (1925).

LOBEL, EDGAR; E. P. WEGENER; and C. H. ROBERTS. *The Oxyrhynchus Papyri*. (Egypt Exploration Society.) London, 1952. (XX.)

LYKOPHRON. Scholia. In: ISAAC and JOHN TZETZES. Λνκοφρονος 'Αλεξανδρα το σκοτεινον ποιημα. Edited by M. C. Gottfried Müller. Leipzig. 1811. 3 vols. (I.)

MALINOWSKI, BRONISLAW. *Myth in Primitive Psychology*. (The New Science Series, I.) New York, 1926. (Psyche Miniatures, General Series, 6; London, 1926.)

MANN, THOMAS. *Freud und die Zukunft*. Vienna, 1936. (Cf. tr.: "Freud and the Future." In: *Essays of Three Decades*. Translated by H. T. Lowe-Porter. New York, 1947.)

MENODOTOS. Cited by ATHENAEUS (q.v.).

MONTFAUCON, BERNARD DE. *L'Antiquité expliquée et representée en figures*. Paris, 1719. 5 vols. in 10. (I.)

Mysteries, The. (Papers from the Eranos Yearbooks, 2; ed. Joseph Campbell.) New York (Bollingen Series XXX) and London, 1955.

NAUCK, AUGUST. See AESCHYLUS, Fragments.

OCELLUS [OKELLOS]. Ὤκελλος ὁ Λευκανος περὶ τοῦ παντός, *oder des Ocellus von Lukanien Betrachtungen über die Welt*. Edited and translated [into German] by H. W. Rotermund. Leipzig, 1795.

ONOMAKRITOS. Fragments. In: OTTO KERN (ed.). *Orphicorum fragmenta*. Berlin, 1922.

ORTEGA Y GASSET, JOSÉ. *The Revolt of the Masses.* New York, 1932.

OTTO, WALTER F. "Der ursprüngliche Mythos im Lichte der Sympathie von Mensch und Welt." *EJ 1955,* XXIV (1956).

————. *The Homeric Gods: The Spiritual Significance of Greek Religion.* Translated by Moses Hadas. New York, 1954; London, 1955.

PHILIPPSON, PAULA. *Untersuchungen über den griechischen Mythos: Genealogie als mythische Form.* Zurich, 1944.

PHOTIOS. *Lexicon.* . . . Edited by S. A. Naber. Leiden, 1864–65. 2 vols. (I.)

PINDAR. *Odes.* In: *Pindari Carmina cum fragmentis.* Edited by C. M. Bowra. (OCT.) 2nd edn., Oxford, 1947.

————. ————. Translated by Richmond Lattimore. Chicago, 1947.

PREUSS, KONRAD THEODOR. *Der religiöse Gehalt der Mythen.* Tübingen, 1933.

PROBUS. Commentaries. In: SERVIUS. . . . *Grammatici* . . . (q.v.).

PROKLOS DIADOCHOS. Scholia on HESIOD's *Erga kai Hemerai [Works and Days].* In: THOMAS GAISFORD (ed.). *Poetae minores graeci.* Leipzig, 1823. 3 vols. (II.)

REINDHARDT, KARL. *Aischylos als Regisseur und Theologe.* (Sammlung Überlieferung und Auftrag. Reihe Schriften, 6.) Bern, 1949.

————. "Vorschläge zum neuen Aeschylus." *Hermes* (Wiesbaden), LXXXV (1957).

REITZENSTEIN, RICHARD, and H. H. SCHAEDER. *Studien zum antiken Synkretismus aus Iran und Griechendland.* (Studien der [Kulturwissenschaftlichen] Bibliothek Warburg, [Hamburg].) Leipzig and Berlin, 1926.

ROBERT, CARL. *Die antiken Sarkophagreliefs.* Berlin, 1890–1952. 7 vols. (III, pt. 3.)

ROGERS, NEVILLE. *Shelley at Work: A Critical Inquiry.* Oxford, 1956.

SÉCHAN, LOUIS. *Le Mythe de Prométhée.* Paris, 1951.

SERVIUS. *Servii Grammatici qui feruntur in Vergilii Carmina Commentarii.* Edited by Georg Thilo and Hermann Hagen. Leipzig, 1881–1902. 3 vols. (Probus in III, fasc. 2; Servius in III, fasc. 1.)

SHELLEY, PERCY BYSSHE. "Prometheus Unbound." In: *Complete Poetical Works.* Edited by Thomas Hutchison. Oxford, 1934.

SIEGMANN, ERNST. *Literarische griechische Texte der Heidelberger Papyrussammlung.* (Veröffentlichungen aus der Heidelberger Papyrus-Sammlung, N.S. 2.) Heidelberg, 1956.

SOPHOCLES (SOPHOKLES). *Antigone.* In: [*Plays*]. With an English translation by F. Storr. (LCL.) 1912–13. 2 vols. (I.)

——. *Oedipus at Colonus.* Ibid. (I.)

STAIGER, EMIL. *Goethe.* Zurich, 1952–59. 3 vols. (Especially I.)

THEON. Scholia on Aratus. In: ERNST WILHELM THEODOR MAASS. *Commentariorum in Aratum reliquiae.* Berlin, 1898.

THULIN, CARL O. *Die etruskische Disciplin.* Göteborg, 1906–9. 3 vols. (II: *Die Haruspicin.*)

——. *Die Götter des Martianus Capella und der Bronzeleber von Piacenza.* (Religionsgeschichtliche Versuche und Vorarbeiten, 3, part I.) Giessen, 1906.

TISCHBEIN, WILLIAM (ed.). *Collection of Engravings from Ancient Vases of Greek Workmanship . . . in the Possession of Sir Wm. Hamilton.* Naples, 1791–95. 3 vols. (III, pl. 19.)

Titanomachia ("The War of the Titans"). Fragment 6. In: *Epicorum graecorum fragmenta.* Edited by Gottfried Kinkel. Leipzig, 1877.

——. Fragments. In: *Hesiod . . .* (q.v.).

TREVELYAN, HUMPHREY. *Goethe and the Greeks.* Cambridge, 1941.

TZETZES, ISAAC and JOHN. Scholia. See LYKOPHRON.

VIRGIL (PUBLIUS VIRGILIUS MARO). *The Aeneid.* In: [*Works*]. With an English translation by H. Rushton Fairclough. (LCL.) 1929. 2 vols.

——. *Eclogues*, or *Bucolics.* In: Ibid. (I.)

WELCKER, FRIEDRICH GOTTLIEB. *Die Aeschylische Trilogie Prometheus und die Kabirienweihe zu Lemnos nebst Winken über die Trilogie des Aeschylus überhaupt.* Darmstadt, 1824.

——. *Nachtrag zu der Schrift über die Aeschylische Trilogie nebst einer Abhandlung über das Satyrspiel.* Frankfurt am Main, 1826.

WHITE, NEWMAN IVEY. *Shelley*. New York and London, 1947. 2 vols. (II.)

WOLTERS, PAUL HEINRICH AUGUST. *Das Kabirienheiligtum bei Theben*, I. Arranged by Gerda Bruns. Berlin, 1940. (Only I published.)

XENOPHANES. Fragments. In: DIELS (q.v.).

INDEX

INDEX

A superior figure indicates a note on the page cited.

A

Academy, at Athens, 58
Achilles, 109 ff.
Africa, 70, 73 f.
Agamemnon, 109, 111
Aischylos, 23, 25 [9], 32, 49, 49 [31], 64 ff.,
 78, 91, 93, 108, 111, 125, 126
    WORKS: *Argonauts*, 82; *Glaukos of*
 Potniai, 66; *Kabeiroi*, 82; *The Persians*,
 66; *Phineus*, 66; *Prometheus Bound*
 (*Prometheus Desmotes*), xxiv, 34, 39,
 56, 64, 65, 75, 78, 79 ff., 83 ff., 101,
 118; *Prometheus Delivered* (*Prome-*
 theus Lyomenos), 66, 67, 69, 72 f., 80,
 83, 88, 97, 112 ff., 123; *Prometheus the*
 Fire Bringer (*Prometheus Pyrphoros*),
 66, 67, 69, 74 f., 75 f., 78, 83; *Prome-*
 theus the Fire Kindler (*Prometheus*
 Pyrkaeus), 66, 69 ff.; *Suppliant Maid-*
 ens, 39
Aither, 25
Aitnaios, 58
Ajax, 109
Akmon, 25
Alkman, xxiii
Alkmene, 40
animals, 88 f.
ankylomêtai, 37
Anthropos, 3
Aphrodite, 30 f.
Apollo, 120, 125, Pl. XII; A. Agreus, 125;
    A. Loxias, 100
Apollodoros, 120
Apollonios Rhodios, 26 [13]
"archetypal," xviii f.
Archytas of Tarentum, 20
Argos, 54
Arkinos of Miletos, 24
ash wood, 46
Asia, 35, 56
Asia Minor, 29
Asklepios, 128, Pl. XIV

Asope, 35
atasthalíê, 27 f.
Athena, *see* Athene
Athena Asia, 56
Athenaios, 82 [14], 127
Athene, 28, 56, 128, Pl. XIV; Pallas A.,
    10, 28, 58, 59; *see also* Minerva
Athenians, 74
Athens, 58, 59, 100
Atlas, 27, 34, 37 f., 119, Pl. VI
Attica, 74, 81 [10], 126
Autolykos, 27
Auxo, 100
ax, 55, 59
Axeiros/Axiokersa/Axiokersos, 57
Axiothea, 57

B

Bia, 84
Blixen, Karen, 74
Boll, Franz, 51 [3]
Bolsena, 128
Bronze Age, 28, 73
brothers, two unequal, 36
Browning, Elizabeth Barrett, xxiv
bubbles, 70
bullfighter, xvi, 14

C

Calanice, 125
Cameroons, 70 [3], Pl. XVI
cap, pointed, 50 f.
catastrophes, natural, 19
Catullus, 123 f.
Caucasus, 117
Censorinus, 20
centaurs, 120
Chiron, 120 ff., 126, 127
Christ, comparison with Prometheus, 3;
    comparison with Asklepios, Sôtêr, 128
Christianity, xvii, 43, 107; *see also*
    Christ